CHRISTIAN ETHICS *in a* SECULAR ARENA

Josef Fuchs, S.J.

Translated by Bernard Hoose and Brian McNeil

Georgetown University Press, Washington, D.C.
Gill and Macmillan, Dublin

CHRISTIAN ETHICS
in a SECULAR ARENA

First published 1984

Georgetown University Press
Washington, D.C. 20057

ISBN: 0-87840-411-2

Gill and Macmillan Ltd
Goldenbridge, Dublin 8

ISBN: 0-7171-1370-1

Library of Congress Cataloging in Publication Data

Fuchs, Josef, 1912–
    Christian ethics in a secular arena.

    Bibliography: p.
    1. Christian ethics—Catholic authors. I. Title.
BJ1249.F75   1984   241′.042   84-7964
ISBN 0-87840-411-2

TABLE OF CONTENTS

Foreword

PART I
In a Secular Arena

PART II
Norms for Today

Foreword

Our Western society is secularized to a high degree. To the extent that this society is interested in the good of mankind and of society, it is inspired by moral concern. Christian ethics shares this concern, in that it endeavors to specify "correct" behavior and action in today's society. It does this with a Christian motivation and with the horizon of Christian faith as a specific dimension. Since our society is not wholly secularized, but is also (for example) Christian, believers must go to their task together with other men. Ethical considerations of all people will be significant for the good success of the common undertaking. Has Christian ethics a place and a special significance in a society which understands itself as secularized to a high degree, and which displays no interest in the Christian faith and a corresponding ethic?

The answer to this question is largely dependent on how a secularized world sees and understands the Christian ethic; but also on how the Christian ethic presents itself in such a world. Besides this, one must consider how Christians themselves understand their fellowship and their ethic; there are notable differences between different types of Christian moral self-understanding. It is beyond doubt that some of these self-understandings—the author means those that are false (and precisely *because* they are false)—have no possibility of being a partner in an ethical dialogue in a pluralistic and largely secularized world.

The following essays were written independently of one another, but deal with various aspects of the one problem which has been briefly presented here. The first essay emphasizes that an understanding, even a self-understanding, of Christian ethics is inexact, if one thinks thereby of a more or less "believed" and therefore "positive" and basically passively "accepted" ethics. Against this, a Christian theology of creation will rather uphold the autonomous creative character of a human and Christian ethics of correct behavior in the construction of a human world. Such an ethics is in a position to be a significant element in a dialogue with a secularized society, a dialogue whose goal is to solve some of the grave problems we face today.

The second essay deals with the same question under the aspect of the so-called crisis of values, and attempts to show that Christian ethics itself—though especially when it is seen falsely or one-sidedly—can lead to a crisis of values with regard to the human realization of our world. But it shows also that the Christian faith introduces the "light of the gospel" (Vatican II) as a decisive aid in avoiding a crisis of values and in constructing a world worthy of man.

Hermeneutics, as this term is widely used today, is important for a correctly understood human and Christian ethic of the formation of man's world; for it can help to establish the concrete moral truth in its relationship to formulated norms, while avoiding the false objectivism and subjectivism of which the secular and Christian partners so easily accuse each other. This is discussed in the third essay.

The fourth essay asks how far the moral norms which are considered so important in Christian ethics are or are not truths of salvation. The answer to this question has many consequences, inter alia, for the understanding of the competence and authority of the Church's teaching authority in the case of moral norms of behavior. The question is extremely important for the understanding of Christian ethics, not only for the interested Christian but also for the secular person.

With regard to the problematic of moral norms in Christian ethics, one may next point to a question which is still open within Catholic moral theology itself: are there "modes of behavior that are intrinsically immoral"? Not only non-Christian partners in the discussion, but many Christians too find it hard to attach much meaning to the assertion of "abstract" formulations of this kind.

A further problem: for a dialogue between representatives of Christian and secular ethics about the correct realization of man's world to be meaningful and possible, they must acknowledge the same criteria. Is the "nature" of man and of worldly reality, to which the Christian teaching on natural law has so often attached great weight, such a criterion? If we see a cultural act of man in ethics, then the problem of "nature and culture" must be handled on its own.

A further essay starts from the fact that moral norms for the human construction of the world are both positively established and supplemented by human authorities. We must reflect on the nature of such authority. Christian authority must above all specify in what sense such authority is "divine": "Human Authority—between Sacralism and Secularism." This involves an important question of the Christian understanding of the world.

Along with this understanding of human authority, a further essay deals with the way Christian ethics and Christian faith can deepen our understanding of secular law. The essay was originally addressed to lawyers of quite varied backgrounds and attitudes.

Finally, we tackle a theme that often leads within the Catholic Church to serious tensions. The bishops are responsible for moral questions as the competent authority of the magisterium, even when they have not specialized in any particular way in ethical questions. Moral theologians have to deal with the same questions, as the specialized expert authorities, but without being a competent authority of the Church's magisterium. It is clear that tensions are possible here; and experience attests that these tensions are real. And yet, both authorities should get together to work for the establishment of moral truth. This would be significant for the Christians themselves, as well as for their joint work with their secular contemporaries. The essay "Teaching Morality: Bishops and Theologians" seeks to examine the problematic presented here.

Most of the above-mentioned essays—originally, papers and articles—have already appeared in different languages. The present collection continues the discussion begun in: *Human Values and Christian Morality* (Dublin: Gill and Macmillan, 1970) and *Personal Responsibility and Christian Morality* (Washington, D.C.: Georgetown University Press, and Dublin: Gill and Macmillan, 1983).

Rome, December 1983   JOSEF FUCHS

1. Christian Ethics in a Secular Arena

The very title of this chapter suggests two important difficulties. First, two realities which are not easily defined are related to one another. Second, the arena of today—although extensively secularized—is not exclusively secular; it is also Christian. Nevertheless, it is important to ask how Christian ethics appears in an arena which is widely acknowledged to be secular, and thereby differentiated from a Christian mentality.

Christian ethics has its ultimate foundation in its belief in a God of creation, that is, a God who is present to everything as its innermost and supportive basis, a God who reveals himself in Jesus of Nazareth as savior/deliverer of a person who is shown to be selfish and considers himself self-sufficient. From this point of departure, Christianity has developed throughout its history a normative ethic with regard not only to personal goodness, but also to rightness of action within society. In so doing, it has also taken on elements (although filtered) from other sources—especially, in the early years of Christianity, Judaic, Hellenistic and Roman sources. Yet a single, unanimous Christian ethic does not exist: there are differences between the Catholic and other Christian versions, as well as differences within Catholicism. I shall refer to Christian ethics from my perspective as a Catholic theologian, in the manner in which I, together with many others, understand this ethic.

With regard to the secular arena I can only refer, at least explicitly, to the Western world. This secular arena rejects a relationship to the God of creation and salvation, and sets itself apart from a normative Christian ethic, which it regards as somehow positivistic. But while setting itself apart from Christianity, it nevertheless stands in relation to Christianity. The secular arena is *not* completely independent of Christianity and is to that extent essentially post-Christian. This secular arena speaks of ethics, however, and largely refuses to be considered unethical. Nevertheless, it refuses to accept any code of ethics merely because it is offered.

Insofar as people of both a Christian and a secular understanding are forced to coexist and to create society together, communication is necessary because of inevitable mutual expectations with regard to those problems which we term "ethical." The question is: What is the relationship between Christian ethics and the secular arena? How do they understand one another? How do they understand themselves, and how can each make itself understood to the other?

I wish to discuss, first, a few basic ethical questions; second, problems of a concrete ethic; third, the discovery of concrete norms, with the problem of "reason-faith," concepts which I shall explain later; and finally, consequences for Christian ethics in the secular arena.

I. BASIC ETHICAL QUESTIONS

1.   Years ago, the Dutch Bishops stated that without faith in God, morality and ethics were impossible; the agnostic Dutch Humanistic Association protested. In spite of their agnosticism, humanists pursue ethics and recognize explicitly in ethics an absolute which they call a "mystery." A few years ago the sociologist and philosopher Max Horckheimer of Frankfurt, also an agnostic, demanded a theology—evidently without God— which would declare that the abundant injustice in the world cannot be the last word. Theologian Karl Rahner has insisted for years that if someone—even if not a professed believer in God— cares deeply for humanity and human values, he clearly acknowledges an absolute. An ethical trend in Poland in recent decades, represented by humanists, Christians, and Marxists, states that the phenomenon of morality as an absolute, an "ought," is a primary, irreducible, and ultimately spiritual, fundamental experience of every human being. Only the attempts at explanations are different—without God or with God, understood with a God as lawgiver or with a God from whom is derived an ultimate meaning and a basic hope of human reality as a whole. A Christian form of transcendental theology sees in the innermost, still prereflective, and also ethical self-awareness of the whole person the inescapable condition of each categorial (including ethical) self-realization in space and time.

Here I simply mean to say that ethics and ethical discourse are possible not only among professed believers in God precisely because of a most profound ethical experience of mankind, and this in spite of those essential differences in basic concepts which still remain.

2.   Earlier, I alluded to the difference between ethical goodness in personal self-fulfillment and the ethical rightness of horizontal actions in the world. The ethical question of the relationship between Christian ethics and secular society, above all, refers to the human (and hence, ethical) rightness of concrete behavior in the world of humankind. This worldly rightness occurring between persons is called "ethical," because the individual ethical person—precisely because of his ethical goodness—will and must interest himself in right conduct within the world of human beings (for morality in the narrowest sense appeals to one's fulfillment as a person). Therefore, in what follows, we will turn our attention to ethical acts and deeds in the world, viewed by (both) Christian ethics and the secular arena.

The question, then, is this: What is the role of Christian ethics with respect to the human condition in a society which views itself as largely secular? To be sure, normative Christian ethics is of no significance to the secular representatives of this society, if it appears to be essentially an ethics of commands, or in some way a positivistic ethic. Is it that? How is Christian ethics viewed in secular society, and how is it understood within Christianity itself?

II. PROBLEMS OF A CONCRETE, NORMATIVE ETHIC

1.   Contrary to the opinion of some nonbelievers and also, unfortunately, of some Christians, Christian morality should *not* be viewed as an ethic of commands. This comment applies equally to the decalogue of the Old Testament and to the Sermon on the Mount of the New Testament. The use of the word "command" is less interesting than what can be conveyed by that term. The decalogue does not attempt to impose commandments; these were inferred by the social-ethical interpretation of Israel and her neighboring peoples. The observance of basic social rules of community life was rather to be for Israel the response to the formation of God's covenant with His people.

The decalogue is to that extent a reminder—an admonition directed toward realization of the well-known social-ethical order. Likewise Jesus' Sermon on the Mount is not a code of commandments but is more a reminder supporting non-egotistical conduct, an opening of persons, of themselves, to others in the world: so it is not a code of commands. This reminder does not confront and challenge humankind with additional commands, but confronts and challenges the sinner, i.e., the egotistical inhumaneness in humanity. In its comment upon certain norms of the Jewish tradition, the Sermon on the Mount tries to urge fuller ethical understanding of what it means to be human. Through paradoxical ethical formulations it forces people away from self-enclosure back toward a fundamental opening of themselves to their fellow human beings. Only an understanding of the complete and concrete reality of persons (and not, by way of contrast, the insufficient formulations of old traditions, or, as I hasten to add, certain natural law formulations of today) can lead to right solutions of the problems of human society.

The epistles of Saint Paul also are largely an exhortation to follow widely known standards of right human conduct that had been previously acknowledged in the moral norms of the Old Testament and in certain Hellenistic ethics. It is in the light of these norms, and in the light of the tradition of Jesus, that solutions to certain new kinds of conflicts are sought. In whatever environment ethical truth is found, Paul reflects upon it and presents it as something to adhere to. Yet Paul does not impose a new ethical code. In his ethical endeavors he is no doubt restricted by his own times as well as by his social concepts. For example, what he thinks about slavery and the social status of women no longer corresponds with more developed and contemporary ethical thought. If we can value some of Paul's comments concerning concrete ethical questions, we gladly follow him. However, the rather brief ethical code that emerges from these letters does not ipso facto represent a universal truth (a code to be followed in all cases) just because it is based on Paul's writings.

The same could be said of the Christian ethic which has developed through the ages. Precisely because such an ethic cannot be and is not intended to be a positivistic ethic of commands, a change is possible—due, for example, to social change and our expanded scientific knowledge in the areas of marriage and sexuality, for instance, as well as to changes in human and ethical value systems. Examples of this can be noted throughout the history of Christian ethics—for example, with regard to slavery, the social status of women, usury, and religious freedom.

Presumably, one often speaks of a certain command structure of Christian ethics because of the importance attributed to traditional teaching and, above all, to ecclesiastical pronouncements regarding ethics.

Tradition and official position-taking have, to be sure, great significance within the Christian community. However, it should first of all be understood that concrete ethical norms are not divine revelation. They do not become divine revelation by virtue of traditional or official teaching. They are the discoveries of human beings, accepted by Christians. Second, I know of no concrete, ethical formulation among those not divinely revealed norms which has been presented by a Church authority as definitive and to be accepted unconditionally. Third, I think that such an authoritative formulation is impossible, since ethical norms, including those of Christians, originate from human evaluation and insight. They are therefore accessible neither solely to authority nor solely to tradition, but to Christians and non-Christians, to bishops, theologians, and laypersons alike. Nor are they accessible only to certain periods of history. Traditional and authoritative pronouncements are significant in Christian ethics, but they are not the *only* important elements.

2.   The basic characteristic of Christian ethics is not an ethic of commands, but the Christian belief in creation, cleansed and deepened by faith in salvation. Creation means we are both set free and commissioned to develop ourselves. Within the very belief in creation is contained the human mandate to develop oneself, that is, to bring one's self from the stage of a primitive beginning to a greater evolution of the reality brought about in creation. That reality set free by creation is to be transformed from its natural state to a state of culture, actively by human understanding, insight, endeavor, planning, reflection, judgment, and effectiveness. Ethics is among the greatest cultural achievements of humanity. There is, however, a distinction to be noted: some make the transition from creation to culture and ethics, and do only that, while others do so and are at the same time aware that they thereby respond to the Creator of humankind.

Jesus of Nazareth has not altered this conception. He does not come to establish a superhuman code of ethics of behavior in this world, nor does he come to substitute for our efforts to come to know moral right and wrong in the human reality of this world. He comes for something other and greater than this. He comes in order to liberate man from an inhuman selfishness, to bestow on him a freedom which makes it possible not only to seek and find ethical truth but also to fulfill it.

To be sure, it has become customary to speak of "God's commandments" with respect to right action for transforming and developing creation. This can be understood correctly, but there is a danger of interpreting it in a positivistic kind of creation theology. When this danger is not avoided, Christian ethics becomes meaningless for the secular arena.

3.   There is a further difficulty in the dilemma posed thus far; it is epistemological in nature. For, in spite of its fundamental belief in creation, Christian ethics, and above all, official Catholic ethics, has the reputation of representing thoroughly absolute norms in the sense of being universal, inflexible, and without exceptions, at least in such areas as body and life, sexuality and marriage, and lying or falsehood. Each of us knows examples. Yet a question arises as to whether and to what extent such "absolute" formulations are justified on the basis of creation theology and the gospel. In any case, Paul, in spite of his faithfulness to the word of Jesus regarding marital fidelity, believed that this fidelity was not required in a special conflict situation, that is, in a case in which the value (as established by the word of Jesus) of marital unity endangered the higher value of one's Christian faith. Thus, in this example treated by Paul, if one partner of a previously non-Christian marriage becomes a Christian and the other cannot tolerate such a change "and desires to separate, let it be so."[1] Paul is not thinking here—as we formulate it today—"deontologically" (or in absolute terms) but rather "teleologically" (or in terms of goals).

A well-known, rather conservative theologian considers abortion justified in a few extreme cases, but does not admit any significant reasons as justifying contraception, which is a much less significant intervention. In the one case he is, like Paul, thinking teleologically; but in the other case, he is thinking deontologically. This seems inconsistent; but it is understandable on the basis of a very specific way of looking at natural law. This theologian perceives the proper performance of the marital act as prescribed by nature (that is, ultimately, by the God of creation) and therefore as binding and without exception, but he has a different optic on abortion.

Within Christian ethics one sees more and more, as in the aforementioned case, an erroneous interpretation of humankind and nature as divine creation. The nature of particular natural abilities and characteristics (for example, in the area of sexuality) offers "laws of nature" only in the sense of physiological, biological, and psychological laws. These laws do not indicate *how* human beings have to take these data into account within the *totality* of human self-realization: the reasoning powers of humans must discover that. This is demanded by the nature of human beings as persons. The physiological nature willed by God indicates only what it is, not how it is to be lived. The being (the "is") does not, as such, contain the category of the "ought," nor does it by itself indicate "what" ought to be done. The being delivers directly neither the categorical imperative nor that which is to be done. In this sense it is not entirely proper to speak of the "sacredness" of human life and of natural faculties, for such a formulation already connotes something ethical, something about right and wrong.

We could say the same thing concerning discussion of the refusal or bestowal by God of rights over human life. There is no such code of rights granted by God, there is only the God-given reality of human life. Just and thereby justified intervention in human life is found only by human reflection about men and human society.

It should be obvious that the human obligation to foster cultural development does not mean an arbitrary disposing of created realities. It deals with responsible human reflection upon the nature (or creation) of human reality. Therefore I do not like to speak of exceptions in the realm of established ethical norms. A normative proposition, which under certain foreseeable circumstances must allow for an exception, is not yet adequately formulated to be universally applicable. One might compare the normative word of Jesus on marriage to the judgment of Paul. Therefore one would not actually require exceptions; rather, with the help of norms, we should seek objectively right solutions. This is known as right reason ("recta ratio"). In brief, on the basis of difficulties on the part of persons attempting to formulate them, acceptable and prima facie right norms are largely inadequate, that is, one is perhaps not justified in applying them universally; for they do not yet take into account the entire reality of concrete data.

If we forget this limited character of many universally formulated norms, such norms are hardly intelligible for the secular arena and for some Christians. Furthermore, it would be better to be more cautious in formulating official and nonofficial explanations of concrete Christian ethics.

III. THE ESTABLISHMENT OF CONCRETE ETHICAL NORMS: REASON AND OPTION

1. According to creation theology, referred to above, the obligation to foster cultural development demands the self-discovery of the human being, and this includes the ethical rightness of his horizontal actions in his world. This corresponds to both the humanistic and the secular understanding of ethics.

As we seek norms for ethically right behavior, we reflect (with evaluative reason) upon the entire reality of human existence. We reflect upon the insight already attained into the nature of man and the nature of ethics; we reflect upon both personal and societal experiences regarding human behavior. We reflect upon hypothetical projects and their possible consequences, etc. All of this is meant to help us discover the better human way toward realization of this world. If it is found, it has to be considered as an ethical—and in this sense, absolute—obligation.

This reflection is often not done in an explicit way; it does not occur without reasons, even when it does not originate expressly *from* these reasons. I wonder whether such an inexplicit reflection precedes every explicit ethical reflection. It seems to me that this is probably the case. To be sure, the inexplicit reflection can therefore lose its significance in the course of explicit reflection. Why is this so? Because explicit reflection becomes aware of difficult conflict situations that challenge the purity of the initial reflection and of the theoretical problems behind them.

According to what criteria should one make moral judgments based on this reflection, especially this explicit reflection? That question is dealt with by many ethical systems; even Christian ethics has problems with this. Nevertheless, in practice, one frequently arrives at good, commonly accepted solutions in spite of the remaining theoretical differences. The concrete awareness of criteria may be greater than the theoretical. I am convinced that further discussion between all those interested is a true possibility, even if commonly accepted theoretical results are seldom produced.

2. The dialogue between Christian and secular partners concerning the right realization of human society should be made possible, in principle, because of an appeal to human reason. One may ask: can the Christian partner in this dialogue really appeal equally to reason? A frequently heard opinion states that it is not the Christian partner, bound by his faith, who is the steward of reason, but that partner who is bound by no option—let us say, the secular philosopher. Let me quote Bruno Schüller:

> [Many Christians think that] genuine philosophical ethics is only what the others, that is the non-Christians produce . . . Some moral philosophers think that it is not "convenient" to deal with theological ethics. You may meet philosophers who will really be of the opinion that among theologians theonomous moral positivism is the normal doctrine.[2]

The view to which Schüller refers is clearly in direct conflict with the conviction of the Second Vatican Council. The Council requires that the Christian work toward jointly reasoned solutions to human problems with his non-Christian partner,[3] even if the Christian undertakes his reasoned consideration "in the light of the Gospel."[4] Is that a problem?

Two points must be considered here. First, the "light of the Gospel" does not consist of solutions to problems, but rather provides a guiding light for the purpose of expanding human insight.

Second, it is said that the Christian partner in the debate is tied to certain positions because of his faith. But I think the positions of secular thinkers, of the agnostic, the skeptic, etc., are equally not simply evident, but contemporaneously personal options. The thinking of the non-Christian is also the thinking of a person who has made basic options. Moreover, all thinking about ethical questions is influenced by the personal disposition of the thinker and seeker. It remains critical that reason be required to provide justifying reasons in deciding ethical truth in spite of various options of faith or personal disposition on the part of the Christian or the secular thinker. There is no thinker who is only a thinker. There is no ethicist who is solely an ethicist. Therefore, the duty is incumbent upon both partners in the debate to listen to one another and to speak to one another in order ultimately to distill legitimate reasons and solutions without prejudice. That is even more important with ethical questions, since they pertain not only to logical but also to value insights. There is a question here of a process of reciprocal liberation and direction.

IV. CONSEQUENCES FOR CHRISTIAN ETHICS IN THE SECULAR ARENA

I hope I have shown that it does not necessarily follow from the various basic concepts of man and ethics that there need be a dichotomy in the phrase, "Christian ethics in the secular arena." The problem originates more from the perception that many have of this ethic as a positive code of ethical norms prescribed by God or by the Church, and seen as being absolute, unchangeable, and universal. A sympathetic investigation into an ethic understood in this way, that is, as an all too "sacred" ethic, appears impossible to the secular person, and rightly so.

1.   The fact that Christian ethics is seen so often in this light is due to an insufficient and erroneous understanding on the part of some "simple" Christians, incorrect information they have received, as well as to some public positions, both official and unofficial. There is a real need to inform others in a thoughtful, adequate manner, devoid of apologetics or polemics. Moreover, there is a need not to demand too much of the Christian to whom the message is addressed. The formulation "This is God's command and the teaching of Christ, which we cannot compromise" requires a more farsighted application, if we in the secular world are going to share in a common pursuit of the truth and the well-being of man; but that is precisely the intention of our faith in creation.

2.   A deeper explanation of the ethically significant teaching regarding the God of creation and man as creation, as well as of the true ethical significance of the mystery of Christ, can condition a Christian ethic, which still would not have to be something foreign in the secular arena. It would preserve true

human ethical autonomy and creativity, even if not in the sense of a totally independent arbitrariness.

For Christians this (relative) autonomy and creativity, based on the theology of creation and salvation, will have a special meaning: they understand, both as human beings and as Christians, that they are the bearers of the (human) development of humanity, the transcendence of which is always immanent. Herein lies a profound and urgent motivation for ethical engagement. Precisely for that reason they join past and present. That which arises from their inner Christianity as well as from their non-Christian exterior is drawn into their contemplation, examination, and judgment.

3.   In their human and Christian attempts to find help for the formation of human reality, the representatives of Christian ethics see themselves, to be sure, not only on a par with their secular neighbors, but also influenced by specifically Christian ideals in the fulfillment of their mandate. The "light of the Gospel" offers no concrete ethical solutions, but it does offer important basic insights for ethical understanding. Among these insights are the truths about creation, man as sinner, salvation and freedom, and the call to divine and eternal life (in spite of "being sinners") in which we see the ultimate depth of the dignity of each individual human being. To this "light of the Gospel" belong also the maieutic and parenetic emphases, for example, on love. Also pertinent are the quasi-paradoxical examples of the Sermon on the Mount which advocate genuine, total openness of the true human being, and this in contrast to being a sinner. Finally, there is the radicalization of those ethical demands so often formulated by persons in a reductionist and minimalistic way. If Christianity in this light has always been on an ethical quest, in reality it was nevertheless only half successful in reaching a conclusion, not infrequently because of the insufficient sensitivity and openness of Christians. Therefore Christians must again and again place themselves under the light of the Gospel, in order to seek, in an enlightened way and together with secular persons, the true path to humanity's complete realization.

4.   If Christians, in the light of the foregoing reflection, attempt to discover the truth about the right human realization of human existence, they must bring the best of Christian ethics to

their attempt to promote the right self-realization of human society. Humanity needs this. But Christians should not rank as divine revelation or as the teaching of Christ or even as the irrevocable doctrine of the Church what in reality does not belong to these three categories. Furthermore, they should not force things on others because of wrongly supposed "Christian" sources. It is much more important to make oneself and the accepted values intelligible and to promote them.

Whoever views Christian ethics in the manner in which I have attempted to portray it might also consider it plausible to promote it within the political realm of a pluralistic society, which is, after all, expected to serve humanity. Christian ethics should not strive to have itself protected by laws of the state; that is not the role of the state. However, it should strive for democratically promulgated laws and regulations which follow, as far as possible, the direction of those human values and of a truly human ethic, which appear to be convincing. In this way it intends and tries to support man, human society, and human order.

Christian ethics distinguishes between the realm of transcendence and faith, on the one hand, and the realm of the inner-worldly, horizontal realization of man, on the other. While it makes such a distinction, it is aware that both realms exist simultaneously in the same one person, and that each realm is significant for the other and moreover influences it. Even so, Christian ethics does not forget that the Christian brings to reality the realm of faith and transcendence not only along with, but also largely through the investigation and horizontal realization by man, and often not in an explicitly reflected manner. The more clearly Christian ethics delineates these differences for itself, within the community of believers and also within the largely secular society, the more unbiased it can be in trying to affect society; and non-Christians, for their part, will be inclined not to hesitate in accepting the contributions of Christians to society.

NOTES

1. 1 Cor. 7, 13–16.
2. B. Schüller, "Zur Diskussion über das Proprium einer christlichen Ethik": *Theol. und Phil.* 51 (1976), 321–343, on p. 337, fn. 28.
3. Especially in the Constitution *Gaudium et spes*.
4. *Gaudium et spes*, no. 46.

2. *Christianity, Christian Ethics, and the Crisis of Values*

It has become commonplace to talk about the crisis of values in today's more or less secularized society. Many Christians hope that Christianity can and will become a help, a bulwark, and a port of salvation in the midst of this crisis. My purpose is not to speak on the many and varied reasons for this crisis; rather, I will propose, under three headings, some reflections on certain aspects of the relationship between Christianity—and especially Christian ethics—and the crisis of values today.

First, I intend to indicate certain understandings of Christianity, and Christian ethics, that I consider rather erroneous or at least one-sided. There are understandings that I think will not be a help in this crisis of values, but rather a danger, at least indirectly.

Second, I will argue that Christianity, if it is rightly understood, does not avoid every danger of a crisis of values, for such a danger is intrinsic to Christianity itself.

Third, I will suggest that Christianity, if it is rightly understood, does nevertheless offer substantial help against the crisis of values and can help in overcoming this crisis.

I. ERRONEOUS OR ONE-SIDED UNDERSTANDINGS OF CHRISTIANITY AND THE CRISIS OF VALUES

There are certain understandings of Christianity—and especially Christian ethics—which are inadequate and which appear to be a danger with regard to the crisis of values. It is a pity that such understandings are often presented as "the tradition" and therefore as "the truth"; consequently, they are easily and deeply rooted in the minds of many convinced

Christian believers. Such understandings are in a certain sense "maximalistic" and tend to be rather "apologetic"; nevertheless they do not truly correspond either to the Bible or to today's best theological research. Precisely because they are maximalistic and apologetic, rather than realistic and true, they become the reason for an increasing lack of confidence for many non-Christians as well as Christians with regard to every Christian discourse on values.

1. Erroneous or One-Sided Understandings of Christianity and Christian Ethics.   First, there is a certain fundamentalist and verbalistic biblicism in some understandings of Christian ethics. These understandings are inclined to see divine revelation in every word of the Bible, as far as values and morality are concerned, and this in the sense of either distinctively Christian teaching or at least divine and definitive moral teaching. This biblicism endures even though the biblical sciences today can show that there are no convincing foundations for this sort of biblicism. For the biblical sciences show that many texts have to be considered not as proper axiological and moral teachings, but rather as so-called parenetic discourse, which means a reminder and an exhortation to live the Christian life according to the moral norms which were held in biblical times and according to certain ideal "models." Exegetes also show that certain evaluations found in the New Testament are conditioned by social situations and historical understandings in times different from ours. Finally, they show that in the New Testament some evaluations are probably conditioned by the hope of an imminent eschatological end to this world.[1] When one contrasts a fundamentalist biblicism with these findings of the modern biblical sciences, it is not difficult to understand that someone might despair about the possibility of a valid proclamation of values in the name of Christianity—at least for today.

What has been said regarding an erroneous biblicism could be said, analogically, with regard to an all too static interpretation of the tradition of Christian moral teaching.

Second, there is another understanding with regard to values and moral norms which is not wrong in itself, but which nevertheless creates a confusion between "Christian values" and "values of Christians." This is particularly the case with respect to norms for the right realization of the individual, of interpersonal relationships, and of society itself in this world. "Christian values" should be values and moral norms that belong exclusively to

Christians. "Values of Christians," on the other hand, would not be exclusively Christian values, but properly human values in the best sense of this word—meaning values for all human beings, and precisely therefore also for Christians. But we must not disregard the fact that some Christians often speak one-sidedly and erroneously, I feel, when they present the values "of Christians" as though they were distinctively and exclusively Christian values—distinct, that is, from truly human values. There is a danger in this understanding, for there are many Christians who cannot identify themselves with a system that intends a life of values and moral norms that are "distinctively Christian." Understandably, they regard such a life as being at odds with a Christian life that fosters, in company with other highly ethical men and women, the true values of man and of humanity, while also fostering faith and fidelity to Christ in and through these values.

Third, it is not only a "metahuman" and therefore an "ahistoric" Christian conception of values and moral norms that is in danger of generating a lack of confidence and therefore a crisis of values; one should also take into account the fact that certain types of so-called "human" understanding of values also run this same risk.

I would like to offer two reasons for this thesis. First, sometimes even the so-called human understanding of values remains all too one-sidedly "metaphysical," "static," "acultural," and "asituational." Such an understanding could cause a fear that such an ethic cannot really be applied to the concrete human reality, which is historical, cultural, and situational. If this is so, this so-called "human understanding of values" will not be an understanding that could truly refer to the concrete Christian person. Both the self-understanding of man and his moral experience, even if they are authentically human, are nevertheless never purely nor abstractly human; they are, instead, also conditioned by specific concrete and cultural realities. For instance, the value "marriage" (as we can see, for example, in different periods of the Old Testament), as well as the values of the "interpersonal relationship" and "fertility" of marriages, can change according to the specificity of different civilizations and cultures.

There is a second reason for my thesis. Certain values, whether or not they have already been discovered in an explicit way as true human ideals, and therefore as authentically human values, can be at certain times "not actual"—either "not yet" or "not anymore"—and this may be the case either at a certain point in the development of a culture, or perhaps also in a given situation in the development of an individual human life.[2] For example, certain ideal values in our understanding of marriage today may not be "actual," that is, truly "evident," in certain economic and social situations of some African tribes. This could also happen with regard to certain recognized values which would not be "actual" in certain highly conflictual situations in the lives of individual human beings—for instance, in marriage.

We cannot close our eyes to the fact that some excessively static understandings of human values can be found in discourses on values (discourses that call themselves Christian), and that these understandings could create an aversion and a lack of confidence when some Christians speak of values.

2. *Consequences of Erroneous or One-sided Understandings: A Lack of Confidence.* Briefly, I have said that certain erroneous or one-sided understandings of Christian or human values could generate a rather generalized lack of confidence regarding systems of values which are authoritatively and traditionally proposed.

In this regard we should note, first, that it makes no difference whether we speak of a distinctively Christian teaching or of an authentically human doctrine. There is simply the general difficulty of accepting the idea that certain theories could be used effectively to evaluate and judge human realities because all too many of them are ahistorical and asituational, and this is precisely because human realities do not remain abstract, but are, in fact, concrete.

A lack of confidence may also be engendered if theories on human or Christian values are developed as "theistic" theories. This refers to theories that are proposed as stemming from "the nature" of human reality, insofar as this nature means "creation," and furthermore as stemming from the redemption of this created nature, insofar as the redemption is a reaffirmation of God's creation. Such theories try to say that our attempt to learn from this created and redeemed reality allows us to "read" rather passively the will of God regarding values and the respective moral norms. And, insofar as the will of the eternal God is supposed to be "eternal," all the values and moral norms of natural and redeemed reality will be understood as participations in this "eternal law." Those who hear such theistic explanations of human values and moral norms can come to fear that these norms could not adequately satisfy the real concrete dimension of their lives.

A first consequence of this could be that persons who no longer have sufficient confidence in our teachings on values and norms will feel "free" to do anything whatsoever in certain situations—free, therefore, in the sense of a freedom without limits—and this would mean that they would decide for themselves in the concrete situation about value and norms, always beginning their considerations from zero, considering the concrete reality to be evaluated here and now without given criteria. This would surely be a danger, for one would be attempting to generate opinions and to justify choices which are not well founded and therefore not really "human." Thus, a lack of confidence regarding traditional theories, which are one-sided or erroneous, could incline us to similar attempts at moral reasoning, which would then mean a crisis of values.

There is a second consequence, similar to the first one, regarding the crisis of values. We find today among many people, including Christians, the phenomenon of a so-called autonomous moral experience. The following is the problem: there are many people who seem to evaluate concrete human reality directly for themselves, rather independently of given value systems, and they seem to be able to do this sufficiently well, realistically and reasonably. This experience of autonomy (which is not totally erroneous, as I will show later) brings with it a factual pluralism of evaluation and norms. This could be so either in one's own personal life, or in comparison with the experiences of other persons who live in different situations.

II. A TRUER UNDERSTANDING OF CHRISTIANITY AND CHRISTIAN ETHICS: THE PROBLEM OF "CHRISTIAN VALUES" AND "VALUES OF CHRISTIANS"

We will attempt to find an approach that is a little different from the approaches cited thus far, an approach that is more realistic and truer to the problem of the relationship between the Gospel and values.

1. The Gospel and Values—Christian and Human. Contrary to what we sometimes hear, the Gospel is not primarily a revelation of a system of values or of a code of moral norms for the realization of man, of society, and of the world; rather it is, first of all, the proclamation of the kingdom of God, of His lordship reestablished in this world. This lordship means both a call and an offer to man to change—a call and offer made to man who by himself and without redeeming grace is an egoistic sinner. It is a call to and offer of sincere conversion and opening to God and to one's neighbor, to society, and to the world, and therefore to the true values underlying the realization of worldly reality.

This proclamation/call/offer, which we call redemption, contains a "yes" from the God of Love to the man who, as has been said, by himself would be lost, and this precisely insofar as he makes himself an egoist and in this way alienates himself from his true being—that is, from his innermost meaning as creature of God and brother to his neighbor. Redemption gives back to man and abundantly confers on him his dignity as person, both created and redeemed.

This renewed affirmation of man's personal dignity (though he belongs to the reality that is called "the sin of the world"[3]) entails that God leave it up to man, while yet demanding of him that he understand himself (in society and together with other men) as the image of God and that he therefore understand human values, either as such or as they correspond to given situations—situations in different cultural epochs and situations of the concrete here and now.

It becomes clear, therefore, that the God of Christians does not create or reveal a distinctively and exclusively "Christian" system of values, or a complete system of "human" values for the realization of man and of his world. It is, rather, the task of man himself (of the whole of humanity), created and redeemed as he is, to try to discover the human values and corresponding moral norms for man's required self-realization. The more sincere the fulfillment of this task of humankind is, the greater is the hope of discovering values and human norms that are authentic and true. These values and norms, precisely because they are authentically and truly human, as has been said above, are values and norms for Christians too, and are necessary for their task of realizing worldly life, society, and the world.

Furthermore, because these values and norms are human, they cannot be simply values and norms that are always metaphysical, ahistorical, "actual," and quasi-given from the outside and forever. For these values and norms must also authentically reflect the factual fullness of the historical, concrete, cultural, and situational reality of man, of humanity, and of the world. Certainly in this respect we must also consider the distinctively Christian reality of the self-communication of God.

According to Vatican II's formulation,[4] we are witnessing the birth of a new humanism, according to which man defines himself with respect to his responsibility for his brothers and sisters. According to St. Thomas Aquinas,[5] God will not be offended by anything except by what man does against his own well-being.

2. *"Parenetic" and "Maieutic" Discourse.* The God-given task of all humans, including Christians, is to try to discover human values and corresponding moral norms; this task is, in fact, presupposed by what we read in the Bible regarding values and moral norms. For many relevant texts of the Bible do not intend, first of all, to reveal or to teach values and norms imposed from outside. Their twofold scope mainly concerns something else: namely, the parenetic and the maieutic. Both confirm the task and the real possibility for human beings to discover, on their own, values and norms for their self-realization.

The parenetic scope means exhortation. In fact, the Bible, instead of revealing and teaching a system of values and imposing them on us, mostly urges us to realize presupposed values, i.e., human values that can be known from other sources. The Bible does this for a variety of reasons. The decalogue demands fidelity to the covenant by God's chosen people—a fidelity to be shown precisely through conduct indicated in the decalogue. This conduct was already known by both the people of Israel and the people of the surrounding areas as conduct that was morally demanded. Similarly, the Sermon on the Mount, instead of teaching a distinctively Christian code of commands, expects that the man of the kingdom of God—that is, the liberated and redeemed man—manifest a conduct and behavior of "openness," i.e., a behavior that is human in its best sense. This means an openness to God and to one's neighbor that is not satisfied with the juridically deduced commands of first-century Judaism. St. Paul as well often demands in his letters to early Christians that they do not do what they themselves know to be contrary to true human values and corresponding moral norms— values and norms, therefore, which are already known without the benefit of St. Paul's teaching. The fulfillment of these norms is, according to the apostle, a condition for entrance into the kingdom of God: *this* is St. Paul's teaching.

The maieutic scope consists in the explicit affirmation of certain extremely high values, for instance, love of neighbor and also of one's enemy; this explicit affirmation serves to help man in the difficult task of discovering the highest and most demanding human values and norms. In the examples and words of Jesus and St. Paul, etc., today's Christians can see what Christians of former times understood to be elements of an authentic "humanism," elements that are able to express and to instigate Christian faith. Similar elements derived from Jesus and St. Paul may eventually help us to discover values and corresponding moral norms in accordance with the human reality of our time.

Our conclusion is, therefore, that the preaching of values and concrete norms in the New Testament is mostly not a new teaching but has rather a parenetic and maieutic task. Furthermore, it should not be overlooked that parenetic and maieutic preaching was not done systematically, but only occasionally and sporadically.

3.   Absoluteness and Relativeness of Values.   The explanations just offered would lead us to understand that even those values and coresponding norms that are called "Christian" will also be "human" values and norms. These norms and values determine the building of a more and more truly human world. It is clear that these values and norms that are discovered and understood by ourselves, including ourselves as Christians, manifest to us something of man's true reality.

It will be important, therefore to distinguish between those values and norms that are values and norms for man simply as such, and therefore always and everywhere normative (for instance: truthfulness, fidelity, a certain culture of sexuality, the high value of the institution of marriage), and those values and norms that we discover and understand as corresponding to special cultures and situations (for instance, as corresponding to a specific, socio-economic reality).

These considerations should, first, provide the basis for our confidence that we will not be manipulated in actual situations by those somewhat ahistoric ideas of a system of values; second, they should provide us with an assurance that we would not forget man as such, even in concrete moral circumstances.

Surely this poses a problem. There is in moral theology a tendency to retain, at any cost, all the judgments on values and norms from the past, precisely in those instances in which one thinks that these judgments are altogether "eternal" judgments.

Many of these judgments, especially those that are more concrete and operative, suppose specific cultural or situational facts, and, consequently, cannot belong as such to other times and places. St. Paul's ideas on slavery, for instance, and on the status of women in society, are perhaps understandable for his times, but they do not convince people of our society, and will not be considered as eternal, therefore, but rather as related to a humanity and society that are different from those of today. The social ideas of Pope Leo XIII's *Rerum novarum*, which were so progressive in the last century, were no longer satisfactory for Pius XI, the pope of the encyclical *Quadragesimo anno;* and the ideas of the latter encyclical are considerably surpassed by the documents of Popes John XXIII and Paul VI, and by John Paul II's *Laborem exercens.* The obligatory value of justice is eternal; the manner of realizing it in the concrete is not eternal in the same sense. A consequence of this is that even if we do not feel obliged to accept, without distinction, all the evaluations and norms of other times or of a certain tradition, this does not yet amount to a real crisis of values, for truthfulness, fidelity, authentic social justice, and a truly human understanding of sexuality are needed at all times.

The fact remains that the so-called autonomy of man, or of humanity, in discovering values and norms, brings with itself the danger of "manipulation" of values and norms. For, on the one hand, man remains always a very limited being in his attempts to discover values and norms, and, on the other hand, he easily deceives himself when he follows desires, fashions, ideologies, etc. In this respect, his greatest opportunity for discovering human values for himself (both those values we call eternal and those that are conditioned by cultures and situations) is all too easily actualized in a self-deceptive manner; this, then, is a true crisis of values.

III. "THE LIGHT OF THE GOSPEL" (VATICAN II)[6] AND THE CRISIS OF VALUES

While the autonomy of humanity, including that of Christians, is able to free us from the danger of a system of values that is purely ahistorical and thus not very credible, this autonomy can at the same time bring with it the danger of a rather arbitrary system of values. From this consideration arises the question: is Christianity able to help us against this danger? Vatican II, in *Gaudium et spes,* the Constitution on the Church in the World of Today, insists that Christians should search for values—both the so-called eternal ones and also the actual ones of a given historical moment—and that they should do so not only on the basis of the experience of man and the world, but also "in the light of the Gospel." What is the value and importance of the "light of the Gospel" in overcoming a crisis of values? First, a brief and general answer: the light of the Gospel does not simply give us an eternal summary of all human and Christian values; it is, rather, a true help in discovering these values in a correct way, on our own.

1.   Basic Elements of Christianity against the Crisis of Values.   It seems, first, that Christianity's basic contribution against all possible crises of values is the profession of faith in the Absolute, in the personal Absolute, i.e., in a God of creation and of redemption in Christ. This God is the original and absolute source of human values. These values are therefore not only and purely a cultural creation of a totally independent man and society. Furthermore, Christ Jesus of Nazareth is the "firstborn of all creation,"[7] the "firstborn of those risen from the dead,"[8] the "firstborn among many brethren."[9] We are aware that we are the image of Jesus ("of the son,"[10]) and that Jesus is the image of the "invisible God";[11] true Christians will therefore take themselves seriously in order to discover values and norms. In doing so, they remain aware that the values found and affirmed by them, are, in themselves, not values of God himself or of Jesus Christ, but values of human beings. Thus, they are created values, limited values, values discovered by one who is still flesh and not yet totally spiritual—in the sense in which St. Paul uses these words. In searching for and accepting a system of values, men and women of Christian faith in God and Jesus Christ are far different from nonbelievers. Jesus's example of sincerity toward the Father, as well as His behavior, inspires Christians.

Second, faith in an Absolute, in a personal God, has as a consequence the fact that as we come to a true and full realization of man and his world, we will discover many other authentic values of man, including, first of all, religious values. In order to realize himself fully, man must come to acknowledge, revere, and adore the source of his being human and of his being redeemed: God as Creator and Savior. Without the realization of religious values, man has not yet arrived at true self-realization, that is, self-realization in this world. Furthermore, acknowledgment and realization of religious values help in the authentic and sincere understanding of other human values, and give a deeper and unique meaning to their realization.

Third, Christians have a deeper understanding than others of the nature of man's persisting egotistic, concupiscent tendency. This deeper understanding can create in Christians a deep lack of confidence in themselves when they are trying to discover or to affirm their own system of values. This Christian faith, confirmed by daily experience, may cause a continuous conversion and eventually also a revision of those values which had previously been discovered; this is a very important element with regard to the "creative-autonomous" search for human values and in the light of the permanent danger of a crisis of values.

Fourth, Christian faith professes that in the crucified and risen Jesus, the God of creation and redemption has, in generous charity, definitively accepted all men, every man, although man's overall situation remains that of the "sin of the world."[12] This faith therefore gives to believers a vision and evaluation of man that are impossible, at least in the same way and to the same degree, for nonbelievers. In this call to all by God the Creator and Redeemer to an eternal unity with him and with all, is to be found the ultimate fullness of the dignity of the human person. Because a Christian knows this, he must devote himself without superficiality or arbitrariness to the task of discovering a system of values for his own formation as an individual and also for his interpersonal and social relationships, marriage, and sexuality. But the dignity that man recognizes is shared by all persons, whether they be of great or little intelligence, rich or poor, friends, strangers, or enemies. Every individual has such dignity that he should not be instrumentalized, must always be respected, and must be liberated from circumstances of insufficiency, oppression, and so forth.

Admittedly, the concept of love of one's neighbor, whether as an individual or a group, friend or stranger, is not found exclusively in Christianity and in cultures under Christianity's influence. Nevertheless, the proclamation of the dignity of every human person and of the love of one's neighbor in Christianity has had and still has a dynamic and leavening influence. Certainly, even within Christianity itself, many of the consequences of this evaluation of man as the subject of dignity have been realized rather slowly: one thinks of the question of slavery, of social injustices, of the lack of appreciation of the social status of women, of religious intolerance, and of many other oppressions. Nevertheless, it is quite possible to hold, with good reason, that much of the recognition of the dignity and rights of human persons in our time derives, at least partially, from Christian doctrine on the human person, even in circles and places where one no longer speaks of Christianity.

Fifth, it is a matter of no small importance to reflect on the Christian concept of man's eschatological and definitive situation. He who ponders our definitive destiny—that the gift of God's grace is justice, reconciliation, charity, and peace with God and with all of humankind—cannot with moral logic consider himself free from certain consequences. He will feel a continuous duty to attempt to do whatever is possible to create, in advance, an anticipation of that eschatological situation to which all human beings have been called—an anticipation to be worked out not only in our immediate and interpersonal ambience, but also in national and international affairs. Under this aspect, certain theses of current political theologies or theologies of liberation have a distinctive value.

Sixth, the Second Vatican Council's term, "light of the Gospel," also implies our being inserted into a church community. This community is a continuous and common attempt at the realization of Christian faith in human life and therefore of authentic human values. Those who take into serious consideration the Church community—that is, all of its members guided by pastors and still more by the Spirit—have, because of this, a strong orientation which militates against what we today call the crisis of values. This is not to say that either in the past or today the Church community has always and necessarily been in full possession of an exact system of values; the Council itself noted this in the Constitution *Gaudium et spes*. The consequence of this fact is that a somewhat critical commentary on certain aspects of the Church community is not to be totally excluded. But it cannot be denied that we are given by the Church community—in its continuous and sincere attempt to provide direction, orientation, and exhortation "in the light of the Gospel"—certain strengths and enlightenment against the crisis of values.

2. *The Importance of Christian "Parenetic" and "Maieutic" Discourse.*   The foregoing remarks suggest that the parenetic and maieutic discourse—all the exhortations and all the moral teachings of the Bible, of Christian tradition, and also of the Church's present life—have, at least globally, true and great importance. This is so because, as we have explained, they show what other Christians have considered to be values and behavior

that validly express the Christian faith according to human experience and the light of the Gospel. We are therefore, in a certain way, inclined to accept their system of values.

Nevertheless, we have already pointed out that this is true only globally. The reason for this is that a number of elements had an influence in Christian thought in different historic periods. This could be demonstrated in certain traditional evaluations and normative judgments, especially those that are more concrete. Similar influential elements were, for instance, certain ideologies or philosophies (e.g., stoic philosophy), the lack of various experiences and of the authentic knowledge that we possess today (for instance, about the nature and function of money, of biology, physiology, psychology, sexuality, etc.).

The possibility and fact of similar influences brought about by experience and systems of thought should free us, at least in certain cases, with humility and courage from those evaluations and normative judgments of the past that are not well enough founded and therefore not convincing. This freedom should be welcomed, since we have a deep tendency to let ourselves be determined by evaluations and moral judgments of the Christianity of the past. In fact, not all elements of the parenetic and maieutic content of the Church's history are, without exception, eternal and definitive.

3. Christian Dynamism: The "Already" and the "Not Yet". Perhaps the foregoing considerations will lead us to understand, in the light of the Gospel and of the parenetic and maieutic aspects of Christianity, that the most important element, from the early period of Christianity until today, is the continuous and serious effort at discovering a convincing system of values with corresponding moral norms, at least for a certain period. Both a strong conservative tendency and a courageous attempt at correcting those positions that are not well founded, equally manifest this dynamism, through different orientations. In fact, because of our faith and "in the light of the Gospel," Christians cannot live without trying to make their treasures fruitful for the world, for society, for their interpersonal relationships, and for the formation of individuals. The stronger the faith of individual persons, of various groups, and of the whole Church community, the stronger will be this Christian dynamism. This dynamism will lead Christians to evaluate what seems to be already accepted, and to try to discover new human values which have not yet been discovered, along with the correlative moral norms. This could be done either by coming to a knowledge of reality that has not been known until now, or by coming to a new reflection on the evaluations and norms of tradition. This could be done in order to introduce into and to realize in this world the so-called eternal values, as well as actual values of the here and now. This could ensure that the historical incarnation of Christianity in the formation of humanity and of the world would be authentic and concrete.

I would like to add only one thought: I hope that I have not been totally unsuccessful in presenting a rather positive, constructive, and therefore valid reflection on the problem of Christianity and the crisis of values in a secularized world, a reflection that is more valid than certain merely apologetic reflections.

NOTES

1. Cf., for instance, 1 Cor. 7.
2. Thus K. Rahner, in: A. Röper, *Objektive und subjektive Moral. Ein Gespräch mit Karl Rahner,* Freiburg, Basel, Wien (1971), 58: "... values, which because they are not yet actual do not yet actually oblige ... do not oblige even if ... one already 'theoretically' knows the demands which comprise them."
3. John 1, 29.
4. *Gaudium et spes,* no. 55.
5. Thomas Aquinas, *S.C.G.* 3, 122.
6. Vatican II, *Gaudium et spes,* no. 46.
7. Col. 1, 15.
8. Col. 1, 18.
9. Rom. 8, 29.
10. Rom. 8, 29.
11. Col. 1, 15.
12. John 1, 29.

3. Moral Truth—between Objectivism and Subjectivism

In a more or less secularized world, Christian ethics is widely understood as a system of objectively given moral norms, which also determine moral truth in the concrete here and now. For their part, Christians fear that in the ethical systems of a secularized world a subjectivism is at work, leaving behind true objectivity and having sole power to determine the moral truth *in concreto*. Against these two tendencies, as sketched here, the concrete truth is to be seen, in what follows, in its precise position between objectivism and subjectivism; thus, "objective" and "subjective" are not antitheses.

"Moral truth—between objectivism and subjectivism" is a formulation that can be open to two kinds of criticism. The reason for this is that "moral truth" is used in the singular and is distinct from "moral truths" in the plural. On the one hand, one could fear that the normative "moral truths" widely referred to as "objective" and formulated as universally valid and exceptionless principles and norms, could become relativized by subjectivistic understanding in the very search for concrete "moral truth" here and now. On the other hand, there is reason to suspect that in the judgment on a given specific situation, "moral truth" would in the end be prejudiced by preformulated principles and norms and would therefore perhaps not be real moral truth. The question is evidently important for the problem of the "right" realization of our human world.

"Moral truth" is here understood as the moral judgment that actually corresponds to a given, concrete, real, personal situation. This situation (be it real or considered) is, insofar as it is particular, necessarily richer than the reality that is judged in terms of necessarily abstract "moral truths" (principles and norms). The concrete reality may thus contain morally relevant elements that have not yet been sufficiently taken into account in preformulated "moral truths." It is important to point out explicitly that the formula "moral truth" used in this context is not meant to be identical with a similar formula used by Thomas Aquinas[1].

The problem of "moral truth" has its parallel in law. There, the question is what the true "right" is in a given real or imagined situation, with regard to the formulated law: is the true "right" contained exclusively and totally in formulated laws (objectivism)? Or is the true and concrete "right," despite the formulation of the law, to be found and determined by a searching subject, for instance, the judge (subjectivism)? Or is the true "right" similar to the "moral truth"—something that is beyond subjectivism and objectivism?

The problem of the "true right between subjectivism and objectivism" is today an important theme in law. Those who think that true rights are to be found *between* objectivism and subjectivism will refer to hermeneutics. For the sake of simplicity, I should like to refer to an article by Arthur Kaufmann.[3] This chapter will make much use of this interesting contribution.

Because of the analogically similar problem in law and ethics ("true right" and "moral truth"), one could suggest comparing the respective reflections in law and moral theology. But for moral theology and ethics it seems to be more important to accept the suggestions and reflections in law in order to consider more explicitly the similar problem of "moral truth."

I. SUBJECT-FREE OBJECTIVISM?

The problem in law is well known. A widely accepted objectivistic-positivistic tendency is inclined to think that, at least in principle, every right is totally and exclusively contained in the law. Therefore, the judge must bring only the law to the search for the true right; he must keep himself out. Nevertheless, it is agreed that, at least in principle, sometimes a loophole in the law has to be filled. On the other hand, there is the question as to whether or not, per se in every case, the judge (perhaps without being aware of it) has to adapt the law and the case, the two "raw materials," to one another in order to discover the true right in the process of bringing them together. In so doing, the judge would neither objectivistically ideologize the law as opposed to the case, nor subjectivistically sacrifice the law.

1. There have undoubtedly been objectivistic tendencies within Catholic moral theology, for instance, among neo-Scholastics of the last 100 years. Today, too, there are similar tendencies in official Church documents. These tendencies deal to a certain degree with normative moral truths in analogy to positive law. In searching for moral truth, they try to eliminate, as far as possible, the creative power of a subject. Objective moral truths (norms) mean in this context not so much those more or less *formal* principles which are more concerned with personal moral *goodness*: for instance, principles which demand the will to be and to do good, faithfulness to one's own moral conscience, readiness to be just, truthful, chaste, etc. These formal principles, as opposed to laws, do not yet say what has to be done or not done in the concrete. Objective moral truths, therefore, are here understood as those *material* moral truths (norms) which demand or forbid concrete actions. What do justice and faithfulness really demand or forbid in everyday business affairs? What types of sexual behavior actually correspond to or contradict the virtue of chastity, etc.?

One would be surprised to find that the aforementioned objective tendencies in the area of morals exist. For moral truths (norms) are not positive laws. Nevertheless, they have been considered in the past and are also considered today very often and practically in analogy to positive laws: as paragraphs of a law code or as a sum of laws more or less accepted by the Church community and declared as binding by the Church authorities. This, then, is precisely the reason why these moral norms are called *objective*; in fact, like positive laws, they formulate "objectively" an obligatory course of action, a formula that has to be *the* measure for all concrete "cases." But is it not true that in this way the nature of moral truths (norms) is misinterpreted? What does the term "objective" really mean if moral truths are so called? Does it mean that an authority imposes or approves them, or that moral theologians have written so in textbooks, or that these truths are considered valid in society or in a community, either because of agreement of the majority or because of tradition? But this would be precisely a juridical or legal understanding of moral norms. The basis for the objectivity of moral truths is not all this; rather, it is the fact that moral truths truly correspond to human reality, so that they therefore have their value not because of the authority of the hierarchy, or of theologians, or of books, but because they can be evaluated and judged as moral truths *in themselves,* as "right reason," precisely as "moral truth." This is the fundamental understanding of the so-called natural moral law. But in this sense not only moral truths (norms) but also the moral truth of a personal situation must be "objective." This is a parallel consideration to the fact that not only moral truth (in the singular) but also moral truths (in the plural) are discovered and understood in their objectivity by human beings, i.e., "subjects." Therefore, error is not only not excluded in searching for *the* moral truth, but also in searching for normative moral truths; i.e., in both cases it is possible not to reach objectivity.

2.   In regard to the law, it is, in a special way, the judge who has to apply it to actual cases. In an objectivistic understanding of the law, he has to be a more or less "receptive automaton." In regard to moral truths, the application has to be made, first of all, by the acting person himself, who has to come to a decision in a concrete situation of human reality as he sees himself confronted with normative moral truths. But this application must also be done by every counselor, pastor, moral theologian, really anyone who on certain occasions has to arrive at a morally responsible solution to problems which arise in his private and public life. All these people must be more or less "receptive automatons" when confronted by a preformulated system of norms—the parallel of a code of laws.

At least in its use of words, but also to a large extent in spirit too, there was and still is a certain school of moral theology that shows this tendency. This school explicitly understands the search for moral truth (in the singular) as being only the "application of moral truths" in a case considered merely as a number; it therefore calls normative moral truths objective and their application, subjective. Nevertheless, there is (although in a less clear way) a certain awareness of the parallel to the problem of the loophole in laws; a well-known formula states that the manner of applying moral truths has to be "according to the special circumstances of a single case." For in this formula it is implicitly acknowledged that preformulated moral truths do not cover the entire reality without leaving loopholes and that, in searching for the moral truths of the concrete reality, more moral creativity than mere subsumption is needed. This formula in a certain sense does away with the basic problem of moral truth (in the singular), because a moral judgment on the morally relevant elements in the particular circumstances has perhaps not yet, or only insufficiently, been accomplished in the already known truths.

In searching for moral truth, however, it is not enough to see the parallel in the loopholes in laws—quasi a case of exception. On the contrary, what we call simply "application" of normative moral truths has basically and in every case a markedly "creative" character: the subject is always more than a "receptive automaton"; he brings himself much more into the process of finding moral truth in the concrete. The "case," or rather the concrete human reality, is not simply seen "in itself." The reality of the situation is judged by the subject much more as a reality that is already "understood," to a certain degree (that is, understood in the light of moral truths already known), and normative moral truths are always applied in their already understood meaning for the concrete "case." In the personal application it will be discovered whether or to what extent those moral norms, which according to their (human) formulation offer themselves to be applied in the concrete situation, are in reality able to consider the concrete situation as their "case." Maybe yes, maybe no, because the concrete reality possibly contains morally relevant elements which in the abstract formulation of norms have not yet or not sufficiently been considered; but sometimes perhaps the concrete reality does *not* contain such elements (for instance, in regard to the moral norm, "never kill another merely in order to please a third person"). Whoever intends to find the actual moral truth has to bring the aforementioned creativity as subject into his considerations along with already known moral truths and the concrete human reality. Where this is not done sufficiently, there is a danger of sacrificing moral truth to an ideologized norm-objectivism. In fact, we often exercise this creativity, perhaps without an explicit reflection, when we "apply" moral truths. But there are also many cases in which ideologized objectivism and a defect of "moral maturity" (L. Kohlberg) impede the needed creativity and therewith the discovery of objective moral truth.

It should be explicitly pointed out that in a correct search for moral truth, the moral subject does not make himself the measure of truth; rather, he allows himself to be measured, in his creative activity, by the unabbreviated fullness of the reality—the personal-material condition, already known moral truths, the necessity of coming to concrete judgment. This again does not mean that moral truth is found independently of the subject (*subjektfrei*); similarly, neither have normative moral truths been formulated independently of the subject.

II. BETWEEN OBJECTIVISM AND SUBJECTIVISM

Measuring as an understanding subject and thereby allowing oneself to be measured by the reality itself, means that moral truth is neither subjectivistic nor subject-free. The corresponding school of law, which in a parallel manner is interested in finding the "true right," calls on hermeneutics for this purpose. The judge simply cannot approach the law in a concrete case without bringing with him an expectation of meaning, and therefore a precomprehension and a horizon of understanding (not yet a prejudgment). So says Gadamer; Habermas, I think, would add, not without an "interest." It is only because the judge brings with him an expectation of meaning (*Sinnerwartung*) and because therefore his horizon of understanding is basically along the lines of the understanding of meaning incarnated in the law, that both the law and the judge will reciprocally specify their understanding of meaning. In this way, there is a real encounter between the law to be applied and the judge who applies the law. So the true meaning of the law becomes expressed and the true "right" can be found. Therefore, the so-called "hermeneutic circle" just described is not a subjectivistic method, but merely explains the process by which the true "right" will, in fact, be found.

(A brief observation by A. Kaufmann is of interest to moral theology. He adds to his exposition the comment that neither positivism nor a natural law conception are able to explain the fact of the hermeneutic process. This formulation seems in the end to suppose a "positivistic" and "static" understanding of natural law,[3] which undoubtedly could not explain the natural-law way of finding rights (and moral truths, as well as moral truth). But it is precisely in the field of ethics and moral theology that this problem is decisive, as will be shown in the following pages.)

1.   There is undoubtedly a parallel between the relationship "law"-"rights" and the relationship "moral truths"-"moral truth." But the difference between the two areas is also evident: the law has been positively "given" in society (by lawgiving, by tradition, or whatever); and it is therefore certainly binding. Normative moral truths, on the other hand, have not been "given" in this way, despite the fact that this claim may appear—or seem to—in certain religious formulations. Moral truths belong to man's self-understanding (ultimately because he is God's creation); they originate from our human understanding, evaluating, judging, formulating. They are therefore binding not because they have been "given" but because they are conceived as an expression of the right understanding of "being human." In other words, in whatever way man has come to formulate moral truths, these truths are binding not because they have been formulated; rather, they are binding because of their formulated content, though the fact that the content is precisely this and not something else, depends on human understanding and formulating.

The foregoing implicitly suggests that the content is, in principle, open to further human reflection. Moral insight and judgment which have entered into moral truths are therefore also necessarily in relation to the moral insight and judgment that lead to moral truth in the concrete. We have already observed earlier that human insight and judgment are activities of human subjects in discovering both abstract moral truths and concrete moral truth.

Consequently, in discovering moral truth, one is basically always in the stream of moral insights in human history and tradition. Nevertheless, the concrete "application" of given moral truths is fundamentally different from the concrete application of laws. The judge is bound by the law as a reality stated in society (the question of his relationship to an "unjust" law is not to be considered here). The application of moral norms, on the other hand, does not stem from such a binding obligation (not even in the case in which an authority has declared them). Rather, it has to be understood as a continuation of the process of discovering moral truths in the history of humankind (even in the case where moral norms have been declared authoritatively).

Therefore the "application" of laws and the "application" of normative moral truths are fundamentally not the same; nevertheless, according to the foregoing explanations, applications will be made in the moral area too by a hermeneutic process.[4]

The human insights in given normative moral truths, and the single individual subject (or even a group) searching for the moral truth, encounter one another. In the face of a real situation (with reciprocal influence), a mutual understanding and, consequently, a new self-understanding of the searching, concretely situated person will come about. Moral truths are aids in the discovery of actual moral truth.[5] In this hermeneutic process, our knowledge of the experiences and reasons which historically are sources of moral truths are of great importance. In this process it is similarly very helpful to have an understanding of what was ultimately meant or intended in the formulating of norms, even when this was not explicitly stated. Furthermore, consideration of various branches of knowledge (psychological, sociological, historical, etc.) in different epochs is important. But especially important is the understanding of the special circumstances of the situational reality not yet considered in abstract norms. It has already been observed that in this encounter and in the attempt at the hermeneutic translation of already known moral truths into concrete moral truth, it must become clear whether and to what extent a traditional moral formulation is right or wrong, adequate or inadequate, and how it can perhaps be brought to a better and more adequate formulation, so that this formulation can really be a light for the moral understanding of a concrete situational reality.

2.   As opposed to what happens in the application of law, the search for concrete moral truth is ultimately not a question of the "application" of something already "given," but rather the discovery of concrete "moral truth." But this discovery is, at least in principle, directly possible in the same way as the discovery of abstract moral truths. Nevertheless, such a finding of concrete moral truth necessarily has an inner relationship to already known moral truths, even in the case where these have, in fact, served no part in the discovery of concrete moral truth. But this is said knowing that, practically speaking, finding concrete moral truth does not normally happen without a more or less conscious relationship to already known normative moral truths. In finding moral truth, no one is without a relationship to society and to its past and his own. It is precisely, therefore, the hermeneutic translation into the here and now, which excludes both an "objectivistic" subsumption under norms and an isolated "subjectivism," that is always needed.

In addition, the formulation of concrete norms of behavior is also not done without involving the subject in the process of finding moral truths. For such norms of behavior always imply (even if perhaps in an unreflected way) already known, formulated or unformulated, less concrete principles and norms. But because these norms are more abstract than the concrete moral norms, they do not subsume in themselves the more concrete norms. An "extension" is needed which essentially includes both the relation to a more abstract principle and an evaluation not available in advance.

III. THE NONARBITRARY AND THE INDISPENSABLE

If moral truth is to be found neither subjectivistically nor independently of the subject (*subjektfrei*), a question arises as to how, in this way, objectivity will be assured—and this without objectivism. Surely, such a finding of truth supposes that the searcher already knows in a certain way what moral truth formally means. But also needed is awareness that the objectivity of moral truth in regard to the content has to respect the "nonarbitrary," "the indispensable." The question is: in what does this "indispensable" consist—an indispensable which does not in turn condition objectivism? In regard to the true "right," A. Kaufmann raises the question: "Is there beneath the process of finding the true right, an indispensable (*unverfügbar*) element," and what is it? He refuses to consider "nature," conceived rather according to the categories of material and things, as the foundation of immaterial entities such as, for instance, right and person. But Kaufmann also opposes a purely functional foundation of rights according to which the purely functional relationship to society itself becomes "a new natural law." Rather, he considers the human person, with that relationship to persons and things that is essential to being a person, as the element that determines the content of what has to be searched for in the process of finding the true "right." Kaufmann in this way raises questions which are also very important in ethics or in moral theology.

1. It has already been said with regret that moral theology in the past (especially after L. Molina) tried to understand and determine right human behavior by arguing from the concept of the "nature of things"—as, for instance, in the areas of sexuality, marriage, life, person. It still does this in a certain fashion even today, both in the area of normative moral truths and in the area of moral truth (in the singular). This is evident especially in the formula (belonging to a special understanding of natural law) "from the nature of the matter" (*ex natura rei*). That persons are essentially interpersonal and that interpersonality belongs to their constitution, and that interpersonal and societal relationships are not just something added to "being a person," and that, furthermore, particular realities have their true meaning only in the personal-interpersonal realm (so that only within this realm does the relationship between the different goods and values have its definitive meaning)—all this is highly important both in finding normative moral truths and in finding concrete moral truth. It is not possible to discover moral truth only "from the nature of the matter" in the already mentioned sense, for such a procedure eliminates not only subjectivism but all involvement of the subject. It is, therefore, ultimately objectivistic and favors an objectivistic application in the concrete personal situation, as if one were dealing simply with a quantitative problem. So the hermeneutic process is short circuited, and the true discovery of moral truth is impeded.

2.   It is interesting to see that an ultimately objectivistic interpretation of moral objectivity only "from the nature of the matter" easily connects with an extreme opposite view, i.e., a certain way of interpreting moral objectivity as functionalism. It is true that in Catholic moral theology there is no complete parallel to similar phenomena in law. No one explicitly defends the theory that moral objectivity is founded on, and thus legitimized by, the fact that, through observing certain accepted norms, a given society is able to "function well, or at least to a certain degree." But neither can it be totally denied that a certain tendency toward this viewpoint exists—at least where anthropological considerations lead one to insist explicitly on the "well functioning" of certain societies which have accepted certain forms of moral behavior that are rather strange and incomprehensible to us.

It should be obvious that within a functional understanding of moral objectivity many important moral insights and evaluations would lose much of their dynamism in the struggle for more and better humanness. The well-known formula of Thomas Aquinas, that what is morally wrong (before God) is only that which contradicts men's well-being, does not contradict what has been said. For in this formula Thomas understands men's well-being not in a functionalist sense but as the realization of authentic "being human," with its goods and values.[6] (But it should be noted that Aquinas immediately afterward applies his principle in the manner of an "objectivistic" natural law theory *ex natura rei.*)

Nevertheless, there is also found again and again in Catholicism a certain functional tendency in determining what is morally objective. This tendency becomes important in searching for moral truth in the concrete. In the functional interpretation of the true right, the "functioning" of the citizens, for example, conditions the result because only in such conditions is it possible to have a society "free from disturbance." But the functioning of the citizens in this case stems not from their insights but from their conformity. The legitimizing of the law "occurs" here not only *in* a process, but *through* a process. The rightness is identical to the process (Kaufmann). As a certain parallel in morals to this consideration in law, it has been argued that this is the result of a century of neo-Scholastic moral theology: an *objectivistic* understanding of moral rightness (*ex natura rerum*) has become positivistic to a certain degree within the Church community through more and more frequent "authoritative" declarations. Could it be that underlying this fact is the idea that the Catholic Church community, as a moral community, will "function well" only if individual Christians and groups try to get their moral truths less through understanding (if also with suitable help) than by adapting themselves to the declarations of moral truths? So they may simply "apply" them to a single "case," but this means without an attempt, or at least a successful attempt, at having personal insight. Taking this into consideration, there is no denying that responsible and prudent respect for the declarations as a whole can and will be helpful in coming to concrete moral truth.

This tendency, to which we have referred and which is undoubtedly favored by some groups, not only does not serve in the search for moral truths in the abstract and concrete; it also diminishes one's capacity and struggle for moral maturity (L. Kohlberg) in the discovery of moral truth. The real problem of this trend is perhaps therefore not so much objective *truth*, but rather personal *certainty*. Of course, the question involves certainty about the truth; nevertheless, the emphasis is to a great extent on "being sure." This certainty "frees" one from risk; it avoids "confusion"; thus one "functions" more easily. This is true in an analogous way with regard to the Christian community as such, and with regard to their pastors.

Because of this trend, an authentic personal searching and finding "in the process" will be somewhat impeded. True objectivity is not written with a capital "o"; the truth is perhaps subjectively (although perhaps less reflexively) not as highly regarded as is a sure "functioning."

3. With regard to moral truths, one must say that their foundation lies neither in the pure nature of singular realities and

particular fields of realities, understood more or less in a reified sense, nor simply in one's functioning in society or as an individual. This must be said even more with regard to moral truth in the singular. The objective and therefore unconditional content of moral truth is to be understood ultimately neither in regard to singular realities, understood more or less as "things," nor in regard to simple functioning as a model that could ground moral truths. The model that provides such grounding can only be the human person as the most substantial embodiment of human-earthly reality. But the person, in his unique dignity and fullness of being, is not a singular reality among many others; he is, rather, the point of reference for other persons, for society, and for all the other realities that are important for human persons and human society. Right human behavior in this world— "morally right" in the sense of moral truth in the singular—can be understood only as what is right and appropriate with regard to the acting person. This includes a true relationship to others in all their dignity, rights and justified expectations, as well as to the nature and specificity of the various areas of human-earthly realities. For only in this way is the person truly considered in the fullness of his being. Insofar as normative moral truths about the realization of human reality and the world are abstract, they reflect human reality but not its unique concrete fullness as such. Thus these truths can be truly helpful in determining moral truth and can sometimes determine moral truth in a decisive way. But they can (and often do) indicate moral truth only inadequately, and, furthermore, despite the words used, they cannot truly correspond to the concrete reality. The multiplicity of possibilities is clear if we take into account the fact that the person, with his various relationships, becomes real in the process of evolution and historical development.

In confronting various moral truths, the subject who adopts this indispensable criterion of objectivity must consider whether and how far these moral truths are determined by it. He must make this criterion his orientation in reflecting on the particular specificity of the actual here and now.

Normative moral truths are never accessible "purely in themselves," and are therefore never "subject-free," independent of the subject, because we can attain them in principle only through our own active (and in this sense, "creative") understanding and judging. The same must be said about concrete moral truth (in the singular). Furthermore, moral truths and moral truth are, objectively and practically, intrinsically related to one another, and, at least to a large extent, subjectively as well. Therefore the "application" of moral truths to the concrete personal situation in searching for moral truth is likewise not subject-free. So it should not be misconstrued through an objectivistic interpretation. It occurs in a creative hermeneutic process of understanding and translation. This process is not a subjectivistic method, but simply the way in which concrete moral truth is actually to be found. In order to serve unconditional objectivity, the discovery of truth supposes that in every phase of the process this criterion of objectivity is present.

NOTES

1. Thomas Aquinas, *In Eth. Nicom.* L. VI, 1.I, no. 1131, thinks that "the truth of the practical reason" is determined in comparison not with "right reason," but with the "right appetite" of the person. Concerning this, see the interesting study by D. Capone, *Intorno alla verità morale* (excerpt from dissertation, Pontifical Gregorian University), Naples (1951).

2. Arthur Kaufmann, "Gedanken zu einer ontologischen Grundlegung der juristischen Hermeneutik," in: N. Horn (ed.), *Europäisches Rechtsdenken in Geschichte und Gegenwart (Festschrift für Helmut Coing zum 70. Geburtstag)*, Munich (1982), 537–48.

3. Cf. J. Fuchs, "Positivistisches Naturrecht?," *Orientierung* 20 (1956), 113–15, 127–29.

4. Cf. K. Demmer, *Handeln aus Verstehen*, Düsseldorf (1980); G. Angelini, "Molteplici significati dell'appello all' 'esperienza' nella teologia morale," *Teologia* (Facoltà . . . Italia settentr.) 6 (1981), 132–43, on pp. 141–43. (Cf. also a study on the meaning of *epikeia* in regard to moral norms of the natural law: J. Fuchs, *"Epikeia* Applied to Natural Law?," *Personal Responsibility and Christian Morality*, Georgetown University Press, Washington, D.C. (1983), 185–99.

5. Cf. J. Fuchs, "Die Frage an das Gewissen," in: J. Fuchs (ed.), *Das Gewissen. Vorgegebene Normen verantwortlichen Handelns oder Produkt gesellschaftlicher Zwänge?*, Düsseldorf (1979), 56–66.

6. Thomas Aquinas, *S.C.G.* 3, 122.

Excursus.
Hermeneutics in Ethics and Law:
Points of Comparison

The immediately preceding chapter[1] was conceived as a response, from the viewpoint of theological ethics, to a notable essay by the jurist Arthur Kaufmann, "Thoughts on an ontological basis of juridical hermeneutics."[2] It is the intention of the following brief excursus, delivered first at a colloquium of jurists, to work out some points of comparison between hermeneutics in ethics and hermeneutics in law[3] on the basis of those two essays.

1. Hermeneutics must not be understood as a scientific method; rather, hermeneutics endeavors to work out the (transcendental) conditions of the very possibility of understanding language. How is it possible for someone here and now—i.e., in his concretely and personally conditioned circumstances—to understand an already existing life statement, such as a written text, a formulated ethical norm, a law which has been established by vote, etc.? Moreover, when he understands it today, how does he do so without either abandoning his own point in time or else failing to do justice to the already formulated life statement? Hermeneutics, therefore, does not mean the interpretation of a text in the sense of a static meaning, but the translation of a text into the present tense: what does a particular statement of the past say under the conditions of the present moment? Only through this translation can I be consistent with the statement that has been handed on, and remain faithful to it. Mere verbal fidelity would be a material falsification.

The significance of hermeneutics is to be found especially, though not exclusively, in the field of the sciences that deal with understanding—for example, in philosophy and theology, and therefore also in ethics and law. In ethics and law, hermeneutics is significant above all in cases where the concrete *law* is to be established on the basis of given laws, or the concrete *moral truth* is to be established on the basis of already formulated moral principles or norms. This is not, however, exclusive to these cases, for the making of laws and the establishment of moral norms operate always with an already existing consciousness of law and morality, and with the knowledge of how to read hermeneutically the foundations of this consciousness. In this essay, however, I shall restrict myself to the hermeneutical problem of the establishment of concrete law (e.g., by the judge) and of concrete moral truth. In this case, a subject (e.g., the judge) stands between a current law or an acknowledged moral norm, on the one side, and a concrete human situation, on the other; and it is his duty to establish the concrete law or the concrete moral truth, on the basis of his knowledge both of the current law or acknowledged moral norm, on the one side, and of the legal or moral particularity of the concrete human situation, on the other. Must the subject in search of the correct solution simply classify the concrete situation (as if no subjectivity were involved) as a case covered by the existing declaration (law, or moral norm)? Hermeneutics says that a subject seeking understanding, without giving up subjectivity, must understand both the general declaration in itself, and the concrete human situation in itself, and both in their true mutual relationship; only so is it possible to establish a meaningful relationship between the already existing declaration and the given human situation.

2.   In jurisprudence, as far as I know, the dominant stance or tendency, apart from the case of gaps in the law, is still that law which is laid down and in force regulates or contains in itself in principle all concrete law. There exists above all great fear of a judge who would not keep his subjectivity apart from his judgments, but would include himself as well as the law in the task of concretely establishing justice. Naturally, the judge may not put arbitrariness or a very personal scale of values in the place of the law (I cannot discuss here the abnormal case of "unjust" laws, and leave this aside). Against this, hermeneutics says that the genuine administration of justice—the bringing into their proper relationship of law and a concrete situation—is

utterly impossible without an active (and in this sense "creative") understanding and judgment of the full meaning of the law, which takes into account a concrete human situation and therefore goes beyond the wording, the common interpretation, and judicial tradition. If, therefore, the subject who judges is concerned with justice, and indeed with justice under the law, he cannot "merely apply" it; may it not be the case that he brings the law to its correct application *only* by understanding the genuine intention of the law which is not fully expressed in its own words? It may be that many whose task it is to establish and declare law do behave in this way, spontaneously and without adverting to what they are doing—perhaps, indeed, in contrast to the theory they explicitly hold.

In ethics, there is a similar problematic. Let us begin by accepting that there are real or at least acknowledged moral norms, without here reflecting on the problem (which does not exist in this form in the case of judicial law) of the origin of moral principles or detailed norms of behavior. Let me say here only that moral norms are not understood in this case as dictated or indeed imposed *ab extra*, but are rather seen as grasped, and correspondingly formulated, by man himself (or in human society). Inasmuch as they, like the laws, are formulated in generalities, they too must be brought into relationship to the concrete human situation, when it is necessary to establish concrete moral truth. Since there is no prescribed judge in this task of bringing the two into relationship, many influences can be active, seeking, helping, advising, and deciding. In the final instance, though he may take into account instruction and advice, only the one who has to take the decision to act can undertake the establishment of the concrete moral truth on the basis of accepted moral norms. The history of Catholic moral theology—to speak at the moment only of this particular case in ethics—largely maintains across the centuries, as its prevailing conviction, the stance that appears to represent as well the majority opinion in jurisprudence: i.e., that moral norms determine the concrete moral truth through assumed application to the concrete human situation. This means that the aggregate of formulated (or for-mulable) general moral norms contains in itself all concrete moral truth. This stance theoretically excludes hermeneutics.

Yet hermeneutics means the transcendental conditions of possibility for human subjects to establish the moral truth of concrete human situations by reference to moral norms. This, however, is not possible if subjectivity is excluded, i.e., if the subject does not contribute his own capacities of understanding (his already existing comprehension) to the process of the search for moral truth in the reception of moral norms. Only in the mutual influencing of norm and subject, with a view to the actual human situation, is it finally possible to discover what the concrete moral truth is in the light of general moral norms; this accordingly takes place in the deeper understanding of such norms, without excluding subjectivity. Today there is increasing acknowledgment of this stance, which is explicitly conscious of the absolute necessity for the hermeneutical understanding of norms of behavior in the search for concrete moral truth. This does not lead to a (constantly feared) subjectivism in the moral evaluation of concrete human situations in the light of accepted moral norms, but on the contrary, to a greater objectivity.

3. The brief demonstration of the parallels between the problem of hermeneutics in ethics and the problem in law must not and ought not lead us to overlook and keep silent about the differences between the two fields. In a recent article,[4] F. Böckle sees the difference between ethics and jurisprudence as (I should add: especially) the fact that ethics is interested in the regulation of truth for correct behavior, while jurisprudence is concerned, rather, with the settling of conflict and thus with success in relations between men. One can generally accept this.

The laws of judicial regulation are positive statutes within a corporate entity, whether they go back to an explicit ordinance or to a current custom. They are in force as such, in order to serve judicial regulation and hence peace within the corporate entity. To this extent, the administration of justice exists fundamentally "under the law"; this is true at least of the administration of justice and judicial regulation in their fully expressed form—thus not in the same way as "natural law" which is not expressed in statutes, or international law which is not expressed in positive form, etc. In any case, in order to protect the concrete administration of justice, the administration of justice which is contained in laws must be read hermeneutically in accordance with the thesis set out above.

Unlike the concrete administration of justice, the concrete moral truth does not stand so fundamentally under formulated moral norms; above all, it does not stand under moral norms that could be established in positive form. The concrete moral truth is internal to the concrete human situation or to the man in a concrete situation, and is thereby, fundamentally, observable in the concrete situation also.

Moral norms can come from the most varied sources, and can be handed on through the most varied instances, not necessarily only official instances. Inasmuch as they are directed to concrete moral truth, i.e., to correct behavior, they are a possible, valuable, indeed frequently necessary help—but never an "imposed" help—in the establishment of concrete moral truth. They can help in this way when someone who seeks concrete moral truth as a subject undertakes with his already existing understanding a "hermeneutical dialogue" with already existing norms in their humanly and historically conditioned formulation; thus, and only thus, is it possible to discover the profound truth of a norm that presents itself in human formulation for the concrete moral truth. To fear such a hermeneutical reading of the norm and to attempt perhaps "only" to "subsume" is in reality to miss the concrete moral truth, insofar as this is fundamentally aimed at in a norm.

The reference to moral norms, therefore, does not basically look to the observance of moral norms (which have not positively been imposed) as such, but directly serves the establishment of concrete moral truth, and thus the recognition of morally correct behavior. Thus (unlike the law) it does not directly serve the good of society as such, but perhaps does so indirectly, inasmuch as morally correct behavior affects goods within the community, and the correct reference to norms corresponds to a justified attitude of expectation within the community.

The difference pointed out here between the significance of hermeneutics in the fields of ethics and law is considerable; but it should not be viewed one-sidedly, for first, the moral norm too contains a positive and societal element, since even if it is not "decreed" positively and societally, it is nevertheless discovered actively (and in this sense "creatively") and within the society. It therefore stands, humanly and societally, in an internal relationship to the moral truth which is concrete, human, and to be understood within society. Second, the law too, which establishes positive administration of justice, is not a wholly arbitrary decree, but is intimately bound to the human understanding of law and laws; it is here, ultimately, that the concrete law which is to be discovered and declared in each particular case belongs.

There exists, accordingly, a genuine and close analogy of hermeneutics in ethics and jurisprudence.

NOTES

1. J. Fuchs, "Sittliche Wahrheit—zwischen Objectivismus und Subjectivismus", *Gregorianum* 63 (1982), 631–45.
2. A. Kaufmann, "Gedanken zu einer ontologischen Grundlegung der juristischen Hermeneutik", in: N. Horn (ed.), *Europäisches Rechtsdenken in Geschichte und Gegenwart (Festschrift für Helmut Coing zum 70. Geburtstag)*, Munich (1982), 537–48; D. Mayer-Maly and P.M. Simons (eds.), *Das Naturrecht heute und morgen (Gedächtnisschrift f. R. Marcic)*, Berlin (1983), 597–607.
3. On the problematic of hermeneutics in jurisprudence, I refer to the literature cited by A. Kaufmann in his essay. On the same problematic in the field of ethics (especially of Catholic theological ethics), cf. especially K. Demmer, *Sittlich handeln aus Verstehen. Strukturen hermeneutisch orientierter Fundamentalmoral*, Düsseldorf (1980); idem., "Hermeneutische Probleme der Fundamentalmoral," in: D. Mieth and F. Compagnoni (eds.), *Ethik im Kontext des Glaubens. Probleme-Grundsätze-Methoden*, Freiburg i. Br./Freiburg i. Ue. (1978), 101–19.
4. F. Böckle, "Recht und Sittlichkeit. Der Massstab der Sittlichkeit im Rechtsdenken der Gegenwart," in: J. Blank and G. Hasenhüttl (eds.), *Erfahrung, Glaube und Moral*, Düsseldorf (1982), 9–21.

4. Moral Truths—Truths of Salvation?

Ethical dialogue between Christians and their secularized contemporaries is fundamentally possible, especially when it is a matter of the correct or better realization of man's world. The theological question of how far moral truths have salvific significance and therefore a fundamental reference to an official teaching authority of the Church, has no place in this dialogue. Nevertheless, the question thus touched upon has great significance for Christians and for their moral self-understanding—even though, indeed especially to the extent that, they live in the midst of a strongly secularized world.

When moral theologians speak on "moral truths," meaning moral norms, and even more so when some members of the hierarchy write on them, they frequently state that these are "truths of salvation."[1] It is also said that the answer to questions of salvation therefore belongs, in the final analysis, to the charism of the Church's magisterium. This becomes a problem if these pronouncements are made without distinguishing between different types of moral truths. That personal "goodness" and "being a Christian" must show themselves in deeds and actions, that always and everywhere we must tend toward what is good, that our moral decisions should be in conformity with the judgment of conscience: these and similar statements have to do with "salvation" and are, because of this, truths of salvation and consequently the object of magisterial statements. Very often, however, the formula "moral truths" does not refer to this type of moral truths; rather, it refers to concrete behavioral norms concerning social problems, for instance, or the production, stock-piling, and use of nuclear weapons; interpersonal relationships in marriage and family; the actualization of sexuality, etc.

One therefore refers to moral truths with respect to the "right" horizontal realization of mankind's world. But precisely with regard to similar truths, there is a need to explain more exactly in what sense they are moral truths and in what sense they are not. The answer to this question can have important consequences. In this chapter I shall first give the background to the question, second, indicate the problematic character of a particular answer, and, finally, add some ecclesiological reflections on Bible, tradition, magisterium.

I. THE BACKGROUND OF THE QUESTION

1. Everyone who speaks in one way or another about moral truths as truths of salvation knows that there is a distinction between the moral stance of the person as a whole and the decision, for instance, not to say what is untrue or not to interrupt a pregnancy. There should be agreement between the moral stance of the person as a whole and various particular acts; in this sense the philosopher Karol Wojtyla gave his main philosophical work the title: *The Acting Person.*[2]

It is precisely the relationship between the person and his acts that raises the question: which moral truths are calls to salvation and in what sense? That the disposition of the person as a whole in grace is basically man's personal morality and therefore his salvation, has been recognized even by the authors of the declaration of the Sacred Congregation for the Doctrine of Faith, *Persona humana* (1975), in a rather critical statement regarding "fundamental option."[3] Furthermore, this declaration rightly insists that the fundamental option of the person as a whole is not compatible with just any concrete act. The apostle Paul also teaches that the kingdom of God is not compatible with just any way of life in this world.[4] In fact, the person's basic option can be real only in actual realizations of man in this world (as realizations of the basic option) and, secondly, the expressions of morally good and morally evil options will be different from one another, at least in principle. Not all types of actions can by themselves become expressions of the person's basic option.

2. It is precisely because of this relationship that the formula that moral truths regarding human behavior are truths of salvation, is often used without the necessary distinctions being made. And therefore precisely for this reason it is frequently stated that decisions about similar truths are, in the end, reserved to the magisterium of the Church.

3.   These statements raise the problem of when moral truths are to be understood as moral norms regarding "right" acting in this world. This refers to the right mode of "horizontal" realization of man and his world because these moral truths are, at least for the most part, neither revealed nor directly deduced from faith. Rather, we are dealing here with the multiplicity of "natural law" norms and concrete solutions for the right realization of the world. It is indeed a problem that an unlimited number of very concrete truths which stem not from Revelation but from human insight should be called truths of salvation. It is no less a problem that this multiplicity of nonrevealed truths should be, in the strict sense—and therefore without distinction—the object of Church magisterial decisions. For the teaching office of the Church is basically concerned with the truths of salvation, revealed to us by God Himself. Vatican II's Constitution *Dei verbum* makes it clear that Christian Revelation is revelation of salvation. P. Chirico recently stated[5] that, according to Vatican I and Vatican II, the specific task of the Church's teaching office is concerned with *revealed* questions of faith and morals.

I hope that the background both to frequently used formulae and to the problem of this chapter's title has been made clear. We clearly need more and deeper analyses in order to arrive at valid formulations.

II. THE PROBLEMATIC CHARACTER OF A PARTICULAR ANSWER

1.   Salvation concerns the whole person. God's love communicates itself efficaciously as a gift to the human person in Jesus and the Spirit. This efficacy consists in the fact that the (adult) person, who is basically capable of personal morality, opens himself to the self-giving love of God. That is, he accepts this love and responds in faith and love. The personal "being-decided" in faith and love for the loving and self-giving God is one side of the coin, the other side of which we call grace. Salvation is therefore identical to (given) personal moral goodness. For the (adult) human being, salvation is therefore possible

only through the person's being-decided for God, that is, through personal goodness. This being-decided and goodness are, in the end, identical with the person as a whole; they cannot therefore be "seen" objectively (that is, as an object different from the subject), at least not directly: the person is rather aware of himself and his being-decided athematically.[6]

In the area of categorial life, the moral goodness of the person as a whole expresses itself as an inclination of mind, intention, goodwill, etc. The lack of such an intention would be a sign that the person is not "good" and does not live within the realm of "salvation." Personal moral goodness, as intention and will, is, in a negative sense, not being closed in upon oneself; and in a positive sense, being open to the personal God and to the Other. Therefore it is also fidelity to the created self, that is, conformity between decision and the insight of conscience. It is therefore also the will for the "right" realization of the world of man, that is, a realization which is good precisely for man: of the individual, of interpersonal relationships, of society, and of the material world. More exactly, it is the intention to try to find this rightness and, inasmuch as it is found, to realize it. It is therefore also the moral (good) attitude of "justice," that is, the attitude of giving and leaving to everyone what is his due, the moral attitude of "chastity," that is, the attitude of realizing sexuality in a humanly reasonable way, etc. Salvation is therefore the moral goodness of the person as person, given by grace. Salvation as grace brings about the moral goodness of the person. Moral goodness is both effect and sign of the grace of salvation. What can be said about the moral goodness of the person is therefore the truth of salvation.

2. The person realizes himself and his goodness not "in themselves," that is, apart from the realization of the world of man. Rather, he does so in and through the realization of the world. Because he is "good" and within the realm of "salvation," he tries to realize man and his world in a way that is good for a human being. He cannot be content with an arbitrary realization of the world of man; he is concerned with the "right" realization of his world—this means, as I said above, good for man.[7]

The "rightness" of the "horizontal" realization of man's world is therefore quite different from the "goodness" of the "vertical" realization of the person as person. The "rightness" of the realization of the world is not directly and in itself concerned with personal moral goodness. Rightness is concerned, rather, with the question of which way of realizing the earthly data of the world of man is really human and therefore precisely right—both in the abstract and in general, and in the concrete here and now. The question of the "rightness" of acting within this world is not, in itself, a question of the moral goodness of the person, but rather a morally neutral question. What is right for the horizontal human world: going to the moon or not going? What daily timetable best suits a mother who has to go out to work? What kinds of sexual life are appropriate for human sexuality as understood in its totality and in the richness of its different aspects? Can there be an interruption of pregnancy that is the "right" thing to do, taking into account all the rights and needs involved? What, under certain circumstances, is the right proportion between religious and worldly activity?

As can be seen, not all these questions are questions of personal morality (goodness), but questions of the rightness of our innerworldly activity. The problem is: what kind of activity is conducive to the well-being of man and his world; thus, as already mentioned, Thomas Aquinas.[8] Nevertheless, this "rightness" of human innerworldly activity is called "moral" rightness, but only in an analogous sense. For "moral" in its proper and formal sense refers only to persons and their free attitudes and decisions, but, because personal moral goodness contains concern for the well-being of the human world as its moral task, it urges "right" activity within this world; and only because of this relationship between personal goodness and material rightness, this rightness is also called moral rightness. Of themselves, material moral norms of behavior say only what belongs to right human behavior in the various areas of human life; but they add an appeal to the moral goodness of the person to incarnate itself in this world of space and time only through behavior which has been judged as right. Only the added appeal to moral goodness is therefore, in this formal sense, directly moral, and not the judgment on innerworldly activity.

3.   Thus it is understandable why material "moral" norms are so often called "truths of salvation"—because in our innerworldly activity (that is, in our innerworldly incarnation of personal morality) the formal goodness of the person and the material rightness of the action coincide, or should coincide. Because of the importance of moral goodness for salvation, *the whole* of goodness and rightness is called the reality of salvation.

But in speaking that way, one does not make it clear which element of the whole concrete reality is, by itself, the reality of salvation and which is not.

The judgment as to the rightness of innerworldly actions is not directly concerned with salvation. Thus he who realizes all that is "right" in this world and avoids what is "wrong" is not yet, therefore, necessarily "good" and within the realm of "salvation". Perhaps he is an egoist and only wants to be noticed (cf. 1 Cor 13: but, if he does not have love, he is not in the realm of salvation). On the other hand, he who really, as a person, is morally "good," but is not successful in his serious search for "right" behavior and therefore does not incarnate his goodness in right behavior, can nevertheless be within the realm of salvation. For, as already mentioned, salvation does not have a direct relationship to material "right" behavior, but rather to personal goodness—although, by analogy, we call "moral" those norms which indicate primarily the rightness of human actions, and only secondarily make moral demands.

Someone could try to contradict the foregoing considerations by referring to a special understanding of natural law. He would understand rightness, and therefore the material moral norms of innerworldly behavior, as the "moral" will of God, written by God Himself in the created "nature" of the human person and his world. In this case, the morally good concern for the well-being of man and his world would in the end not be precisely this, but would instead be a searching for and finding of the will of God concerning mankind's many-sided activity in this world. This activity therefore would formally be obedience to the will of God, which he makes us understand through the creation of human reality; but disobedience in regard to God would be the direct opposite of personal moral "goodness." The material moral norms regarding "right" activity within the world of man would thus be seen rather as precepts and prohibitions "given" by God. The (horizontal) realization of the human world would be understood formally not as personal concern for the well-being of man as required by moral goodness, but rather as a constant observing of the multiplicity of God's precepts.

But to this counter-reflection there is a ready reply. It has been said that from the nature God created we can learn only what God wanted to *be* (including, for instance, the physical, psychological, biological, etc. "laws of nature"): that is, the will of God as *creator*. Not so the *moral* will of God: how we *ought* to use and develop what God has created can only be discovered through the equally created power of the spirit of man as he attempts to understand the reality of himself and his world. It is clear that the Christian will use this power of the spirit "in the light of the Gospel."[9] Judgment about what we have to do rises from human knowledge and from the evaluation of human goods and values and of their corresponding realization. Such a judgment is therefore primarily not yet a moral judgment in the strict sense; it becomes the morally obliging measure of human activity within this world through the requirement of moral goodness, which includes the readiness to perform right inner-worldly activity.

These considerations notwithstanding, one could be tempted to refer to Thomas Aquinas, because, according to him, "divine precepts" are identical with the precepts of the "natural law," and therefore identical with *recta ratio* (right reason): but right reason is true in itself and therefore objectively, and is therefore the "will of God" and precisely, therefore, "necessary for salvation."[10] This approach would not simply be wrong but it is too global and lacks the necessary differentiations. For *recta ratio* refers both to personal goodness and to the material rightness of innerworldly behavior; this distinction must not be overlooked. Furthermore, even in regard to the right reason of innerworldly behavior, it would be possible to say that it is *secundum se* (or per se) necessary for salvation; but in that case, we should first have to ask *how*—i.e., by which process—the subjective reason obtains knowledge of objective "right reason" and, second, we must determine which elements of the whole complex of the right reason of inner-worldly behavior allow us to speak of necessity for salvation.

III. ECCLESIOLOGICAL REFLECTIONS: BIBLE, TRADITION, MAGISTERIUM

1.   The Bible would, at first sight, give the impression that the many moral norms of innerworldly behavior are, in the strict sense, *moral*, that is, norms of moral goodness, and therefore truths of salvation. In the preaching of Jesus, the oppression of the poor Lazarus by the rich landlord is characterized as "sin."[11] The adulteress hears the words: "Do not 'sin' anymore!"[12] The requirements of the Sermon on the Mount are directed against something that the "pagans," the "tax collectors," the "*sinners*" do;[13] however, he who would be of the "kingdom of God" will

not do this, he will be concerned with marital fidelity, he will—
where this is needed—not insist on his rights, etc. St. Paul says
that the observation of the precepts of the decalogue is important
for those who wish to "be of the Lord."[14] He regards the
observation of the (right) moral norms implied in the Hellenistic
catalogues of sins as an absolute requirement for those who
would enter the "kingdom of God".[15]

If we look more carefully at the Bible, the resulting image
will be different. The peculiar gift of God's love is that he moves
man as person, who by himself would be egoistic and a sinner, to
free conversion,[16] to a free opening of himself before God and the
other (the opposite of the closing in on oneself of the "old
man"),[17] to a free letting oneself be reconciled with God,[18] to a
free dying and rising with Christ.[19] This (primarily transcendental) openness-love, this moral goodness of man as person
in grace, means salvation. Compared to this, everything else is
relative. This does not mean that it is indifferent, but rather that it
is not an element of morality in the strict sense; it is not in itself
personal moral goodness, salvation. Everything else will be
rather "fruit"[20] and therefore a consequence of moral goodness:
he who loves observes the commandments,[21] etc. He, however,
who does what is considered to be sin (sin as trespasses in the
plural) shows that he is a sinner ("sin" in the singular) as person
before God.[22] By themselves neither right nor wrong works
within this world determine either salvation or perdition. Works
do not, by themselves, determine moral goodness and salvation.
But someone who is personally morally good and lives within the
realm of salvation will try to behave, within this world, in the
right way. If someone does not do so, he shows that he (as
person) is not morally good and does not live in the realm of
salvation. Right behavior within this world is, by itself, not yet
moral goodness and "salvation"; rather it is only—*in itself*—an
effect and therefore sign of salvation. The corresponding norms
are not truths of salvation in the proper sense, but only in an
analogous sense. Formulated norms of behavior are therefore not
absolute requirements in the same sense as those norms which
are moral truths not merely in the analogous sense. St. Paul
knows the word of Jesus on marital fidelity; nevertheless, this
word is not a basis for the separation of husband and wife in a
"Christian" marriage in the same way as it is in the case of a
"mixed" marriage.[23] Although we have the word of Jesus,
salvation is, according to different circumstances, compatible
with both types of behavior.

   2. Christian tradition has to make its own contribution in regard to moral truths as "truths of salvation." This tradition is more easily understood against the background of the Second Vatican Council's repeated requirement that Christians should strive to find solutions to the most serious problems of humanity together with non-Christians, also in the "light of the Gospel."[24] At first, these problems will be grappled with not formally as moral questions, but by trying to find a reasonable solution to mankind's needs. Very often the solution we find is nothing more than a provisional attempt inasmuch as, for the moment, no better solution can be found.[25] Sometimes there is no evidence, in the strict sense, that the solution we have found is the right one. Perhaps, after a certain time, we shall discover that the solution found is not the right one, that it will have rather negative consequences, or that it does not sufficiently correspond to true human ideals. Such solutions are therefore, morally, rather neutral solutions to human problems. In order to find solutions we need the real competence necessary to deal with these earthly problems in question, and, furthermore, the capacity to evaluate goods and values for the service of man. Nevertheless, as a consequence of moral goodness, the solutions which have been found to these human and earthly questions will become morally obliging norms of behavior.

   In fact, throughout history, man and Christianity have proceeded in this way. One experienced, knew, believed that there exists a moral obligation to realize man in an appropriate (that is, right) way, as individual, as personal relationship, as society, etc. The question, clearly, is how we can realize society, rights, state, religious institutions, science, sexuality, the parent-child relationship, etc., in a human, reasonable, right way? It is a curious fact that some of these questions are often considered as moral while others are considered not as moral but as human-societal questions. In reality, *all* these questions are first of all human, earthly questions; in fact the tradition has basically dealt with all these questions in this same way. Consequently, anyone interested in moral goodness knew how we ought to express our personal, morally obligatory concern for mankind's well-being. However, this moral understanding was considered valid only for as long as the human, earthly solution found was still considered the right one. When it became clear that the solution was not the right one (for instance, with regard to the function of money, the right to religious freedom, certain evaluations of sexuality and marriage), other solutions now considered as more appropriate would determine the material norms of moral rightness.

An exception was often made concerning those kinds of behavior which, because of a certain understanding of natural law, were considered as written in "nature" by the Creator Himself.

It is our belief that in all searching for moral truths over the centuries the assistance of the Holy Spirit was present, but this assistance does not mean that the Holy Spirit changes the way in which we search for moral truths, and still less does it mean that the Holy Spirit takes the place of the searching person.

3. In considering the question of "moral truths of salvation," the Church as teacher of moral truths becomes a special problem. This is particularly clear if we consider the teachings of the two Vatican Councils, and especially if we take note of a certain uncertainty and vagueness in formulating the competence of the Church's magisterium in questions of morals—as distinguished from questions of faith. This has been shown very clearly in two recent historical studies of Levada and Riedl on the problem of the magisterium's infallibility in regard to moral questions of "natural law."[26]

There is a widespread uncritical opinion that the Church's magisterium is equally competent in all questions of morals, including those nonrevealed norms of "natural moral law." This opinion, formulated in this way, is neither (a) easily understandable nor (b) sufficiently founded in the texts of the Councils.

(a) This should be evident to anyone who has understood that questions about the right action for the horizontal realization of the human world are primarily not moral questions but questions about humanity's concerns within this world. The Church and the hierarchy do not per se have special access to problems of aerospatial, nuclear, genetic, social, sociopolitical, biological, psychological, sexual, etc. questions.[27] The proper or better way of acting in various areas of human life will be determined by human experience, by human evaluation of human goods and values, by human judgment.

The Catholic laypeople *as* Catholics, the priests *as* priests, the bishops and the Pope *as* such, do not have a specific Christian or ecclesiastical competence in regard to these matters. This does not exclude the fact that, because of anthropological implications of the Christian faith and because of Christian tradition, certain human values can be appreciated more easily and more deeply; they are therefore aids to better evaluations within mankind's world.[28]

But in principle it cannot be easily understood, for instance, where bishops get a privileged ability which makes them more competent than Christian or non-Christian laypeople in finding better human solutions to problems which arise in the afore-mentioned areas. There is a problem as to why or how bishops as such can authoritatively impose the right solutions for right actions on Christian and non-Christian human beings who judge responsibly, but differently, from another viewpoint, for instance, about questions of nuclear power or human sexuality.[29]

For solutions to such questions become *moral* norms of behavior only afterward, that is, after and inasmuch as we have found the human solution to the questions of a better realization of man and his world—in regard to truly human well-being.[30] Moral norms of right ("horizontal") behavior contain in themselves presupposed solutions to human earthly problems; the moral norms can be formulated only on the condition that we (already) have the competent and right solution to these problems. The problem would be different if the questions under discussion were, in themselves, *moral* questions (for example, questions of moral goodness), that is, questions which are independent of the other question about which human activity better serves the human well-being (in the full sense of this word) of man as man. What we have said again suggests that per se questions of—in the analogous sense—"morally" right acting within mankind's world are not questions of salvation.

The conclusions arrived at up to this point do not exclude the fact that, in the service of the People of God, the Church's pastors could and should reflect on the problems of humanly right activity—whether as individual, as interpersonal relation-ship or as human society—in order to be able to offer solutions and to bring to the reality of human society the richness of Christian wisdom and a Christian worldview. In doing so, they will remain aware of the fact that they are not specialists in all questions. They will propose as certain, and consequently as morally obligatory norms of behavior, only solutions that are indubitably certain. Otherwise, they will formulate more cau-tiously, perhaps suggesting that, for a given situation, they do not see a better solution than the one they propose—that is, the solution which in their opinion is the right solution.[31] They will indicate that they propose such a solution both because of their concern for man's well-being and as an aid to the moral orientation of the People of God. In formulating their statements, they may consider what Christians in the past thought about the same or similar questions, but they will not accept the solutions of the past simply and only because they think that these solutions deal with moral questions in the sense of questions of salvation; for they are not questions of salvation. They will remain aware, finally, that the questions they are dealing with are not questions of salvation.

(b) The language of official Church pronouncements seems to point in the same direction. Both Vatican Councils use the famous formula that the Church as such is competent "in questions of faith and morals." This formula had a long tradition and was therefore welcomed by the Councils. It is also found in the text of the Council of Trent; but there the terminology regarding questions of morals obviously does not have the same meaning it had in the last two Councils. The already mentioned recent studies of Levada and Riedl show that the exact meaning of "questions of morals" was never explicitly asked for and therefore never clearly defined.[32] Thus, the Vatican formula does not justify far-reaching conclusions. The same must be said about the parallel formula of the Second Vatican Council, which states only in a very general way and without further clarification that the Church preaches the faith that has to be believed and "applied" in moral behavior.[33]

In addition to this lack of clarity in the two Councils' formulations, there is another difficulty stemming from the fact that the most concrete moral questions of moral rightness are questions of the so-called "natural moral law". But these questions, too, at least for the most part, are not found in Revelation; inasmuch as they are not revealed, they are accessible only by means of human understanding, evaluating, and judging.

Nevertheless, the Church magisterium insists—also in the Second Vatican Council—that it is itself competent in regard to questions of the natural moral law. Here the magisterium is evidently not only thinking of *revealed* natural law questions, and furthermore, not only of the most general principles.[34] On the other hand, the same magisterium teaches that the object of its preaching is the "treasure of Revelation," that is, "Divine and

Catholic truth."[35] Moreover, we must take into account the fact that, according to the same texts (in the First Vatican Council, too) questions of faith and morals can be the object of infallible teaching. On the other hand, the Second Vatican Council states that infallibility is coextensive with the "treasure of Divine Revelation."[36] This formulation logically excludes from the charism of infallibility (and therefore also, I think, from the direct competence of the magisterium in its full sense) those moral questions which belong to the "natural moral law" without being at the same time revealed. The First Vatican Council, which used the general and vague formulation "questions of faith and morals," had already taught that the object of infallible teaching is "the treasure of faith," *depositum fidei.*[37] Furthermore, it made an explicit distinction between those moral questions which can be understood naturally and those which God Himself has (also?) directly revealed.[38] The Council was, explicitly, not prepared to identify positively the *res . . . morum* with the whole of the moral order; the reason for this was that the "merely philosophical principles of natural morality [do not belong] in all respects to the *depositum fidei.*"[39]

Ecclesiology normally states that to the questions of *depositum fidei* also belong matters not explicitly revealed but which have such an inner relationship to explicitly revealed truths that the latter cannot be defended without the acceptance of these other (not explicitly revealed) truths. However, it does not seem conceivable that the unlimited number of concrete questions regarding the moral rightness of "horizontal" acting have such a relationship and therefore belong to the competence of the magisterium in the same full sense as revealed truths do; again we could think of such questions as those belonging, for instance, to the biological, aereospatial, and political arenas. The manner in which the 1973 document *Mysterium ecclesiae*[40] speaks about the relationship between nonrevealed truths and truths of faith, does not raise any real difficulties; the same can be said about the corresponding explanation given by the relator, Bishop Gasser, at the First Vatican Council.[41] Besides, the Church throughout her history seems not ever to have pronounced infallibly upon a question of natural moral law that is not, at the same time, revealed. If one or another theologian had thought of defending such an opinion, for instance, regarding the encyclical *Casti connubii* (1930), such an opinion would have had no chance of surviving in the Church.

If we look at the texts of various official Church documents, the following seems to emerge. The Church is aware of her task, and therefore of her competence, to teach and give guidance on questions of morals, not excluding those which are not revealed. In this activity, as in all activity within the Church, she can be sure of the assistance of the Holy Spirit. But this assistance does not necessarily mean the specific assistance that, according to Vatican I and Vatican II, is promised to her and guarantees infallibility under certain conditions when she teaches truths of Divine Revelation. The difference indicated here can easily be understood if we agree, first, that the many nonrevealed truths about the concrete rightness of innerworldly activity are not questions of salvation, and second, that these nonrevealed truths which are not truths of salvation imply merely human knowing, understanding, evaluating, and judging; for without these latter judgments the moral rightness of innerworldly activity cannot be formulated.

(c) Today's theological discussion about the Church's competence regarding nonrevealed questions of the "moral rightness" of innerworldly behavior distinguishes, first of all, between two different meanings of the word "competent." Does it mean that the Church's magisterium possesses, institutionally, a certain competence to guide the Church community? If we use this vague formulation, it is clear that such a competence cannot be easily denied. If, however, competence means a qualified Christian ability to judge on questions of moral rightness, agreement about such a specific ability will not easily be achieved. This is to be said at least regarding the fact that in such moral judgments, knowledge and judgments about human and earthly realities and facts are necessarily supposed and implied. This in no way denies a point already mentioned, namely, that the Church has received from the Gospel a horizon of belief and a series of corresponding anthropological truths which make possible a specific perspective in judging human problems. As a consequence of the foregoing reflections about the possibility of Church pronouncements on concrete moral questions, there seems to be little basis for the opinion that Church pronouncements on the moral rightness of man's behavior in this world could attain infallibility, with the one exception of a case where a human solution proposed in society is in open contradiction to a revealed truth.

There are certain theologians who think that infallibility in similar Church pronouncements must be defended for another reason. According to this opinion, such preaching of the Church for a long and uninterrupted time would imply infallibility. The reason given is the assistance of the Holy Spirit. But these theologians overlook the fact that, first, the promised special assistance of the Holy Spirit guaranteeing infallibility has as its object the *depositum fidei* (including the natural truths intrinsically related to the revealed ones), and therefore precisely *not* those questions of moral rightness which lie beyond this limited field of questions. Second, there is no theological criterion which allows us to determine the period of time within which the Holy Spirit "should intervene." The history of Christian moral doctrine shows that even erroneous moral teaching can persist within the Church for long periods of time.[42] This is more easily understood if one considers that such questions are not in themselves questions of salvation.

From the context of our foregoing considerations, we can conclude that the Church's guidance on the moral rightness of our innerworldly behavior is not without importance merely because these questions are not questions of salvation in the strict sense of the word, and therefore such guidance does not seem to reach the degree of certainty we call "infallible." There are many other facts within the Church which are of great importance to Christians although they are not directly concerned with infallibility and questions of salvation. As with many other questions, here too we can expect true docility and *obsequium religiosum* on the part of Christians. This formula is better not translated unconditionally by the word "obedience" because it is rather a matter of consensus. Here two elements are important: on the one hand, religious docility recognizes presumption as a privilege of the Church's teaching office; on the other hand, the adage, *presumptio cedit veritati* retains its validity. This formula belongs to post-Vatican I theology; consequently, in the last Council, the relator told those bishops who wanted more exact explanation on this point (regarding the rather general formula of *Lumen gentium* (no. 25)) that it is sufficient to consider the teachings of good theologians on this question.[43]

"Moral truths are truths of salvation" is a formula used by a number of authors, but it is a formula without nuances and therefore cannot be accepted without distinctions. It contains in itself the danger of an "oversacralization" which could be harmful both within the Church and to the relationship of Christianity to the "world," especially to a strongly secularized world. Within the Church, it can have as a consequence an authoritative "administration of moral truths" which is justified neither by the Bible, nor by tradition, nor by the Church's self-understanding. Besides, there are some inexact formulations in some pronouncements about this point. With regard to human-ity's task of responsibly developing and forming mankind's world according to faith in creation (and Redemption), this formula can contain the danger of alienation.

If we try to find a better solution to the problem contained in the formula "moral truths are truths of salvation," we must first consider that morality in the strict sense is not directly related to rightness in our worldly behavior but to the attitude of the person and therefore to personal goodness; everything con-cerned with this personal attitude concerns salvation. Morally right acting within the world of man, however, is called "moral" only by analogy to the concept of morality in the strict sense. Second, with regard to morally right acting, we have to consider that it not only supposes a special image of man but also knowledge of human reality within its earthly complexity; for this we need a human competence which neither faith, nor know-ledge of salvation, nor the Church's guidance and teaching can give in a special way. Knowledge about morally right action is therefore not in itself knowledge of salvation; it serves the formation of this world. Nevertheless, it is morally *relevant* for those who live (morally well) within the realm of faith and salvation.

NOTES

1. As an example, I should like to quote G. Ermecke. According to him, moral truths "are reached in the Church as obliging truths of salvation": "Die Bedeutung von 'Humanwissenschaften' für die Moral-theologie," *Münch. Theol. Z.* 26 (1975), 126–40. Therefore, he thinks that the well-known moral teaching of *Humanae vitae* is "a truth of salvation that obliges under sin": "Zur Bestimmung der Lage in der Moral-theologie," ibid., 30 (1979), 33–44, here at 35, note 13. Regarding this opinion, H. Kramer observes in a general way: "Therefore, in a really experienced encounter and even in an encounter which is merely on the thinking level, people believe that this is a matter of Heaven and Hell and that they 'risk' personal salvation from God or perdition": H. Kramer, *Ehe war und wird anders*, Düsseldorf (1982), 53.

To be understood in the same sense is the well-known formula that the Church must decide on all questions of natural moral law for the very reason that all moral norms belong to man's way to his supernatural end, the teaching of which is precisely the Church's task. Thus, among others, M. Zalba, *Theologiae moralis compendium* I, Madrid

(1958), no. 36; in a similar way, formerly, the present author, for example, J. Fuchs, *Natural Law, a Theological Investigation*, New York (1965), 147–49; also *Theologia moralis generalis* I (ad usum auditorum), 2nd ed., Rome (1963), 85; to the contrary now, for example, J. Fuchs, *Essere del Signore. Un corso di teologia morale fondamentale, trascrizione per gli studenti 1981*, Rome (1981), 35, 218–23.

The same idea seems to be present in the argumentation given for the Church's teaching competence in questions of natural law which states that the way of natural law is the way of man's sanctification, and that this way must be taught by the Church; thus, for instance, J. Visser, in: I. Aertnys, C. Damen, and J. Visser, *Theologia moralis* I, Rome (1956), 142f.

The same seems to be said in the frequently used argumentation in favor of the magisterium's competence regarding questions of natural law, which states that natural law is a divine law.

These different formulations fail to distinguish—as the following pages will show—between norms of moral goodness (the way of salvation) and norms of moral rightness; furthermore, they ignore the question of the capacity of the Church—which does not have any new revelation—to make judgments about similar problems. This is a problem seen more precisely by theologians today than in the past.

Therefore, in a sense, we would be justified in quoting Thomas Aquinas on behalf of this identification of "moral truths" with "truths of salvation." Aquinas tries to answer the question of whether the Church precept regarding fasting obliges everyone without exception or not. Although he admits that the observance of a Church precept is, for as long as the precept exists, the will of God, he gives a negative answer to the question. The reason for this answer is that the Church precept of fasting is not necessary for salvation, while the "divine precepts" are necessary for salvation because they are "precepts of the natural law" ("... praecepta Dei sunt praecepta iuris naturalis, quae secundum se sunt de necessitate salutis"): *S. Th.* II-II, 147, 4 ad 1. Thomas does not make all the distinctions which are today possible and necessary. Furthermore, he supposes that the "divine precepts," although they are of the natural law, are known within the Church. It is evident that the observance of "commandments" which are understood as "divine precepts" belongs to personal goodness and is therefore necessary for salvation—in the same way the observance of everything that is and is accepted as *recta ratio* (natural law) would be necessary. Nevertheless, Aquinas prudently adds that they are necessary for salvation *secundum se* (or *per se*). In what sense it is true that *recta ratio* (natural law) is *secundum se* necessary for salvation and in what sense it is not, is the object of the following considerations. The comment on Aquinas can be repeated on no. 4 of the encyclical *Humanae vitae*.

2. K. Wojtyla, *The Acting Person*, Dordrecht, Netherlands (1981).

3. The declaration of the Sacred Congregation for the Doctrine of Faith (Dec. 29, 1975) on certain questions concerning sexual ethics, states in no. 10: "In reality, it is precisely the fundamental option which

in the last resort defines a person's moral disposition." The very question is whether one lives in the state of mortal sin or not; mortal sin is understood as "contempt for love of God and neighbor," and therefore as the opposite of man's "salvation."

4. E.g. 1 Cor. 6, 9f.

5. P. Chirico, "Infallibility: Rapprochement between Küng and the Official Church?," *Theological Studies* 42 (1981), 529–60, here at 532, where he states that the condition for an infallible teaching of the magisterium is that the object be "a *revealed* doctrine of faith *or morals.*"

6. Cf. K. Rahner, "Gnadenerfahrung," in: *Lex. f. Theologie und Kirche* 4, Freiburg i. Br. (1960), 1001; idem, "Reflections on the Experience of Grace," in: *Theological Investigations* III, London (1974), 86–90.

7. Thus, Thomas Aquinas, *S.C.G.* 3, 122: "Non enim Deus a nobis offenditur nisi ex eo quod contra *nostrum bonum* agimus."

8. See note 7.

9. Vatican II, *Gaudium et spes*, no. 46.

10. Thomas Aquinas, *S. Th.* II-II, 148, 4 ad 1; see note 1.

11. Luke 16, 19–31.

12. John 8, 11.

13. Luke 6, 32; Mt. 5, 46f.

14. E.g. 1 Cor. 7, 19.

15. E.g. 1 Cor. 6, 9f.

16. E.g. Mark 1, 14f.

17. 2 Cor. 5, 17.

18. 2 Cor. 5, 18–20.

19. Rom. 6, 5–11.

20. John 15, 1–5; Rom. 6, 22; Gal. 5, 22.

21. John 14, 15.

22. Cf. Rom. 6 and 7; cf. also Rom. 1, 18–32, and 1 John 3, 4.

23. 1 Cor. 7, 10–16.

24. Especially in *Gaudium et spes*, no. 43: "[Laymen] acting as citizens of the world, whether individually or socially, [they] will observe the laws proper to each discipline, and labor to equip themselves with a genuine expertise in their various fields. They will gladly work with men seeking the same goals. Acknowledging the demands of faith and endowed with its force, they will unhesitatingly devise new enterprises, where they are appropriate, and put them into action . . . "

See also: Pastors "[b]y unremitting study [they] should fit themselves to do their part in establishing dialogue with the world and with men of all shades of opinion."

25. Cf. Vat. II, *Gaudium et spes*, no. 43.

26. W. Levada, *Infallible Church Magisterium and the Natural Law*, excerpt from dissertation, Pontifical Gregorian University, Rome (1971); A. Riedl, *Die kirchliche Lehrautorität in Fragen der Moral nach den Aussagen des Ersten Vatikanischen Konzils*, Freiburg i Br. (1979).

27. Cf. K. Rahner, "Grenzen der Amtskirche," in *Schriften zur Theologie* VI, Zürich (1965), 499–520.

28. Cf. the formula "in the light of the Gospel" of the Second Vatican Council, *Gaudium et spes*, no. 46; see also ibid., no. 43. Also, insistently, K. Demmer, "Moralische Norm und theologische Anthropologie," *Gregorianum* 54 (1973), 263–305.

29. The Second Vatican Council explicitly considers, in *Gaudium et spes*, no. 43, the possibility that even different Christians can—from a Christian vision of man—"legitimately" and "with the same conscientiousness" arrive at different solutions to problems: in this case they should enter into "open dialogue."

30. Again, we should quote Thomas Aquinas, *S.C.G.* 3, 122; see fn. 7.

31. Cf. Vatican II., *Gaudium et spes*, no. 33: "In the face of this immense enterprise now involving the whole human race, men are troubled by many questionings. What is the meaning and value of this feverish activity? How ought all these things be used? To what goal is all this individual and collective enterprise heading? The Church is guardian of the heritage of the divine Word and draws religious and moral principles from it, *but she does not always have a ready answer to every question.*"

In no. 43, laypeople are advised to "realize that their pastors will not always be so *expert* as to have a ready answer to every problem (even every grave problem) that arises; that is not the *role* of the clergy."

32. See fn. 26. Cf. also U. Betti, *La Costituzione Dommatica "Pastor Aeternus" del Concilio Vaticano I*, Rome (1961), 639f.

33. *Lumen gentium*, no. 25.

34. Cf. *Gaudium et spes*, no. 89; *Dignitatis humanae*, no. 14.

35. *Lumen gentium*, no. 25.

36. Ibid.

37. DS (= H. Denzinger, A. Schönmetzer, *Enchiridion Symbolorum*, Barcelona, edit. 34, 1967), nos. 3011, 3012, 3018, 3020.

38. DS, 3032.

39. Thus, the declaration of Bishop Gasser as relator of the theological commission (*Deputatio de fide*): Mansi, vol. 52, 1224, a. Cf. Levada, loc. cit., 54; Riedl, loc. cit., 345.

40. *Acta Apostolicae Sedis* 65 (1973), 396–408.

41. Cf. Th. Granderath, *Geschichte des Vatikanischen Konzils . . .* , 3 vols., Freiburg i. Br. (1903–1906); here vol. 3, 475.

42. B. Schüller, "Remarks on the Authentic Teaching of the Magisterium of the Church," in: C.E. Curran and R.A. McCormick, eds., *Readings in Moral Theology, No. 3: The Magisterium and Morality*, New York, Ramsey (1982).

43. Modus 159: "Tres Patres invocant casum particularem, saltem theoretice possibilem, in quo eruditus quidem, coram doctrina non

infallibiter proposita, ob fundatas rationes *interne* assentire non potest ... " The answer of the commission: "De hoc casu consuli debent probatae expositiones theologicae ... " *Acta Synodalia Sacrosancti Concilii Vaticani II*, vol. III, pars VIII, 88.

5. An Ongoing Discussion in Christian Ethics: "Intrinsically Evil Acts"?

Regarding the right realization of this world, there is in Roman Catholic ethics itself a much discussed problem about the value or applicability of the moral norms that "preside" over this realization. How absolute and universal are our formulated norms regarding human behavior in this world? And more precisely, are there "intrinsically evil acts" of human behavior, i.e., acts that under no condition can be "right"? If so, how can corresponding moral norms cope with the actual reality? The answer to this discussion has to do with the place that Christian ethics can occupy in our secular society. The following pages are primarily a sort of "report," but they also indicate the author's answer.

I. LIMITATION TO THE QUESTION

Today's ongoing reflection regarding the problem of so-called "intrinsic evil" (*intrinsece malum*) is concerned first of all with (synthetic) prohibitive norms (in the sense of normative propositions). These norms deal with morally wrong behavior or conduct regarding created goods and values in the innerworldly and interpersonal areas. In such normative propositions, the subject describes (without moral evaluation) a course of action (for example, taking others' private property to enrich oneself) which will be judged in the predicate as morally wrong. The topic is therefore the (material) moral wrongness of our innerworldly behavior and activity, and not the moral goodness (or badness) of the person in realizing such an action (for instance, vengeance or egotism).

This reflection and its specific discussion therefore do not deal with so-called transcendental attitudes. These attitudes determine the person as such and therefore as a whole (and not only the so-called categorial areas of human behavior)—for example, the attitude and intention of realizing good, not evil, to transform Christian faith into a life that is governed by faith, etc.

Second, this consideration does not deal with norms which are indeed categorial, but which are formal and belong to personal morality. These norms demand the personal moral goodness that tends to be morally right in our innerworldly behavior—for instance, "being just," "being chaste," "being impartial," etc. To speak more exactly, these sorts of norms are exhortations rather than norms in the strict sense. For, as in the decalogue, "chaste" and "just" already contain a moral evaluation, and therefore a moral norm such as "you should be just" is nothing more than a tautology. Furthermore, these sorts of tautological "norms" do not propose operative, normative propositions, because they do not indicate what concrete ways of behavior have to do with "being just" or "being chaste."

Third, this recent discussion does not refer directly to norms which are immediately concerned with moral values (and therefore with personal moral goodness)—for instance, norms which prohibit blasphemy (in the strict sense) or inducement to personal moral evil (sin) or injustice, infidelity, etc.

I should like to point out explicitly here that the types of norms not dealt with in the recent reflection and discussion are not norms about the moral rightness of our behavior regarding innerworldly, interpersonal, and therefore created and limited goods and values. There is no discussion, for example, of the fact that the norms of personal moral goodness in the three areas mentioned forbid "intrinsic evil"; the contrary is never "morally good."

II. THE HISTORICAL STARTING-POINT OF THE RECENT REFLECTIONS

In order to give a sufficient explanation for the recent reflections on the theory of *intrinsece malum*, it is important to know what the formula *intrinsece malum* really meant in earlier times. This formula has not always been understood in the same way by moral theologians. But the current discussion refers precisely to the formula of previous decades and centuries.

A study done by J. Murtagh in 1973[1] can be helpful here. According to this study, the distinction between "intrinsic evil" and "extrinsic evil" expresses, first, the apparent difference between "forbidden because wrong" (*prohibitum quia malum*) and "wrong because forbidden" (*malum quia prohibitum*). "Intrinsic evil" means that something is forbidden because it is in itself wrong, while driving one's car on the left side of the road is wrong only because it is positively forbidden.

Regarding this "intrinsic evil," some theologians distinguish three different kinds. Some say that something is wrong in itself either because of the object of the action (e.g., a lie) or because of the absence of a "right" that would justify the action (*defectus iuris*, for example, euthanasia: "because God alone is the Lord of life"), or because of the danger of committing sin involved in an act (*periculum peccandi*): for instance, an unjustified reading of dangerous, obscene, or anti-Christian literature. Other theologians know only one sort of "intrinsic evil": something is "intrinsically evil" because of the object of the action. These theologians call the other two sorts "*extrinsic* (from elsewhere) evil." Still other theologians use the term "extrinsic evil" when the action which is considered as morally wrong, but not under all circumstances (for instance, killing), becomes under certain circumstances (therefore "extrinsically") morally wrong (for instance, "killing an innocent person").

Although there are different terminologies, there is a certain common understanding of what "intrinsic evil" really means. But this understanding involves two elements: an action is called "intrinsically evil" when, first, it is wrong not because it is forbidden, but because it is morally wrong in itself; and second, it is wrong independently of further circumstances, consequences, and finalities, so that this action judged morally wrong cannot become morally right by reason of further circumstances, consequences, and finalities (ends).

Recent discussion deals with this second element of the definition of "intrinsic evil." The problem is that a certain described action is judged to be morally wrong independently of circumstances, consequences, and finalities that would make the action so described and judged, according to a norm, more concrete and specific.

In other words, the problem pertains to whether or not a concrete action, in the context of its total object, can be morally judged by a norm that considers only one basic object of it, and not possible further circumstances, consequences, and finalities.

Some possible examples of this problem are: masturbation, independently of the possible finality of serving as a test to determine one's ability to marry, and abortion, independently of the circumstance that it is done for therapeutic reasons.

The basic idea of "intrinsic evil" seems to be that an action described in its physical reality (for example, killing or masturbation), is said to be morally "intrinsically evil," so that these actions cannot be rendered morally right by any further specific elements. Yet in reality, the object of the action judged as "intrinsic evil" is normally, presumably always, not simply the physical reality of the act, but also its consequences or finalities: masturbation, as physical sexual actualization, is specified through the "circumstance" of being without a partner.[2]

In fact, moral theologians normally accept that the physical act, together with certain circumstances, consequences, and finalities, can be the object of the action judged to be wrong in itself; but they distinguish these circumstances from further circumstances not yet foreseen in the described object of the act. Some of them, in referring to Thomas and Suarez, insist that per se *all* circumstances, which are not only quantitative but also qualitative in nature, have to be considered as an element of the object of the action;[3] but in this last case, the whole discussion on "intrinsic evil" loses its critical complexity.

Briefly, in whatever way one prefers to determine the object of a moral action, the fact that this action is judged because of its object as "intrinsically evil" means that it can never be rendered morally right by any further circumstances, consequences, and finalities.

This historical consideration of the object of an act judged to be "intrinsically evil" has demonstrated that it is not easy to determine exactly and unequivocally what the normative judgment "intrinsically evil" means. This is important for a correct understanding of official Church pronouncements which judge certain actions as *intrinsece malum* without indicating the exact meaning of such a judgment. On the other hand, there are no Roman official Church pronouncements of this sort (if we exclude some brief answers by Roman offices to certain questions in the last century) until 1930, in the encyclical *Casti connubii*;[4] since then, the formulation "intrinsic evil" has been employed more frequently in Roman documents, but never so frequently as in the document *Persona humana* (1975) on some questions concerning sexual ethics, at the very time when reflection and discussion on the concept of "intrinsic evil" had become very explicit.

III. RECENT REFLECTIONS

Recent reflections and critical observations have different starting-points.

1. There is the question as to whether the theory of "intrinsic evil" does not lead in actual experience to almost unintelligible consequences. Thus, one criticizes the opinion that e.g., masturbation is forbidden even when it is needed as a test regarding either a health problem or the ability to marry.

2. Some formal principles are cited that seem to be formulated precisely to avoid certain incomprehensible consequences of the "intrinsic evil" theory. Examples of such principles are those of the "lesser evil," of the "action with a double effect," etc.[5]

3. It is feared that the "intrinsic evil" theory does not satisfy the other principle, *"agere sequitur esse"* (acting follows being), because this principle seems to demand that we respect in our judgment, in an equal way, *all* the elements of the entire act if we formulate a normative proposition that is meant to be objective. For this reason, the studies by P. Knauer and W. van der Marck, as well as those of B. Schüller, J. Fuchs, F. Böckle, L. Janssens, F. Scholz, R. McCormick, and others, have been fundamentally important.

Several moral theologians start from the premise that "moral," in the strict sense, can be referred only to a concrete, realized human act, *actus humanus*, and not to an act presented only in an abstract normative proposition. In this sense, according to J. Coventry,[6] every morally evil, freely realized act (but at the same time, *only* the act), is an *intrinsece malum*. The distinction between morally wrong and intrinsically wrong is therefore not accepted because clearly the concrete, morally wrong act is not determined merely by the object of the act, without considering the circumstances, consequences, and finalities. Similarly, according to P. Knauer,[7] there should be discussion regarding moral evil only in relation to a freely realized human act, *actus humanus*; but this does not exist without concrete circumstances, consequences, and finalities. Only through considering all values and disvalues of an act does one discover whether the evil of an act has a justifying and proportional relationship to its intended good. W. van der Marck[8] insists that the finality (*finis*) determines the specific meaning of an act that is a "human act." Only the finality makes one realize that the removal of a physical organ is either a healing act or an organ transplant and that it is therefore a justified intervention. Consequently, contrary to what has been done in the past, it is not possible to make a moral judgment about the moral rightness or wrongness of the removal of an organ as such. A similar judgment was given by E. Schillebeeckx several years ago.[9]

I think that the considerations by these various authors may make us skeptical about the theory of "intrinsic evil" in the sense in which it was formerly proposed. It is true that these authors are thinking that the concrete "human act" is the only "personally moral" act, in the full sense, and therefore a morally good or morally bad act; but they are interested primarily or even exclusively in the "material" moral rightness of the act according to its object, circumstances, and finality (end).

Other writers (Schüller, for one)[10] begin their analysis by determining moral rightness in a somewhat different manner. Schüller proceeds in a rather formal, almost "neutral" manner. He questions whether a certain way of acting, described by its different components, can be judged to be "right" for our innerworldly and interpersonal life. The rightness of such a way of acting becomes a moral rightness because the personal moral goodness (of the human act) strives to realize itself morally, which is possible only in humanly right actions in the afore-mentioned sense. In other words, the rightness of an act is called "moral" only because of its relation to the personal moral goodness of the action. In dealing with the problem in this way, as many authors do, the question arises of how far an act that is described by its object (with perhaps some circumstances and finalities), independently of further circumstances, conse-quences, and ends can be judged to be wrong in itself, and therefore never justified and thus never morally right. Schüller states that this has been said in the past only by Kant, Fichte, and in Catholic moral theology.[11] Many Catholic moral theologians today are very skeptical of such a possibility.[12]

Obviously, the foregoing considerations recommend the use of traditional moral-theological theories—for instance, the theory of the three sources of morality (in which the object of the act has a privileged position and special relevance in judging the moral rightness of an act, as opposed to the circumstances and the end) and the theory of the act with a double effect (in which certain evil consequences of an act have been considered tolerable only in the sense that they are only indirectly intended).

So the question is: under what conditions is a described act (e.g., killing, contraception, falsehood) so definitively judged that all other conceivable circumstances and finalities remain morally irrelevant with regard to its "rightness"? When is the causing of evil consequences that are inevitable in the actualization of an important good (for instance, the death of a fetus caused by the act of healing a pregnant woman who must otherwise die) so obviously morally wrong that such an evil is justifiable only on the ground of an "indirect intention"?[13]

No one, I think, will doubt J. Coventry's idea that a concrete, here and now morally wrong act is an "intrinsic evil."[14] I believe there will also be a common acceptance of the opinion that, in the abstract too, an act can be described with regard to *all* morally relevant elements, by taking into consideration object, circumstances, consequences, and finalities, i.e., excluding all other possible circumstances, consequences, and finalities, and therefore can also be judged as morally wrong: in this case "intrinsically evil." A frequently cited example is that it is always and (therefore "intrinsically") morally wrong to kill someone merely to please a third person. Nevertheless, such formulations are of little interest because they are so obvious.

But another question is: what is to be said in all the other cases in which an act is not concretized by the addition of circumstances and the exclusive determination of the end—for example, in the case of falsehood, self-killing, contraception, etc? The question theologians ask is not whether such acts are morally right, but rather whether these acts are always and under all known and conceivable circumstances morally wrong, "intrinsically evil." Many theologians today think that it is almost impossible to demonstrate this.

IV. A SPECIAL PROBLEM: "INTRINSIC EVIL" AND THE "DEONTOLOGICAL WAY OF ARGUING"

With regard to the present discussion on "intrinsic evil," the distinction between the so-called deontological and the so-called teleological way of argumentation in moral theology and ethics is very important.

The deontological way of arguing judges the moral rightness of an act independently of the possible consequences to our human interpersonal life; it declares the act in this way "intrinsically wrong," e.g., falsehood, self-killing, contraception, etc. The teleological way of arguing judges the moral rightness of an act according to the "effects" and "consequences" and their "proportion"—as the Church has argued in the past in considering the order of charity or the principle of an act with a double effect. The deontological way of arguing proceeds first of all from the "nature or natural finality of a faculty or act" (*ex natura vel finalitate naturali actus*) or from the "lack of right" (*ex defectu iuris*). Precisely these two types of argumentation are sources of difficulty for those theologians who support the recent reflections on *intrinsece malum*; I think B. Schüller is the guide[15] here. So we must consider these two types of argument more fully than we have already done in Chapter 1.

The first of the two types of argument that have been criticized is the argument from "the nature of the act" or "the natural finality of a faculty" (*ex natura vel finalitate naturali actus*). The argument is well known in the tradition especially with regard to the nature of sexuality and the nature of human language: that is, against the "unnatural" use of sexuality (unchaste acts) and against the "unnatural" use of human language (falsehood, or a lie). The objection raised against this type of argument is that it does not distinguish between the will of God as creator and the moral will of God. It has been said that from the particular nature of an act (for example, human sexuality and human language) it is possible to understand the biological, physiological, psychological, etc. "laws of nature" as the will of God, because these natural laws have been created and are therefore also the will of God as creator. On the other hand, it is said that from the will of God as creator we cannot deduce what is God's will regarding human beings' use of created realities and their use within the whole of human and interpersonal realities: "moral natural law." The *moral* will of God, and therefore a natural law obligation, is not indicated in the nature and the natural finality of a particular act; rather, moral rightness has to be discovered by a moral judgment and this potential has been given by God to human beings.[16] Moral rightness is not discovered through the natural finality of human sexuality or human speech; rather it resides in the capacity of human beings to make moral judgments. There is full agreement that in order to come to a right judgment about human behavior it is important to take into account the particular natural reality willed by God as creator (for instance, sexuality and human speech); what is not accepted is that the consideration of this particular natural reality is enough to make a moral judgment on right human behavior without considering the whole concrete human reality: without considering the relevance of all the elements of the whole of this human reality, it is not possible to arrive at an "intrinsic evil." Therefore, masturbation and falsehood would not be unchastity or a lie, respectively, if there were proportionally important reasons.

The second of the two types of argument is the argument from a "lack of right" (*ex defectu iuris*). This is used primarily in the area of human life and the human body (the fifth commandment of the decalogue), but also in other areas; for instance, to explain certain divine concessions which seem to be against natural law but which are found in the Old Testament. There is again full agreement that the much used formula that "God alone is the Lord of human life and the human body," is certainly right. God is, in this sense, the Lord of all creation. The objection to this way of arguing is that no differentiation is made between God as the transcendent Lord of all creation (and only in this sense is he the Lord) and God considered as a Lord or law-giver in society, who gives rights and reserves rights to himself; but in this last sense, God is neither the Lord of all creation, nor the Lord of human life and the human body. It is therefore said that one cannot deduce anything from the formula "God alone is the Lord of human life and the human body" about the justified or nonjustified disposal of human life and the human body, or about the disposal of other created realities. That God alone is the Lord of human life and human beings means nothing other than that human beings are forbidden to dispose arbitrarily of human life and the human body, according to this understanding; but this is true with regard to the whole created reality of this world. If there is a human right to dispose of human life and the human body, it has to be discovered by a human reflection on the nature of human beings, on the nature of interpersonal relationships, and also on the nature of human society. A deontologically based "intrinsically wrong" would therefore not be possible.

It is important to see that precisely with regard to deontologically based "intrinsic evil," the defenders of this type of argument in the moral theology of the past introduced the famous, already mentioned principles for avoiding unacceptable consequences of such deontologically founded moral norms—for example, the principles of the act with a double effect and of the lesser evil. These principles are not proven deontologically, however, but rather teleologically!

It is interesting to see B. Schüller suggesting that perhaps all the deontologically proven intrinsic evils (according to defenders of these principles) in both of these ways of arguing are really conceived in a teleological way. He suggests that there are some human acts that better serve the well-being of human beings and humanity than do other acts. He also thinks that those who use the two types of argument mentioned understand in reality that nobody knows this better than God himself, the creator and foundation of nature and rights; and therefore they try to discover whether God has not indicated in the created reality itself what may be the better or the right activity of human beings in this world.[17]

Finally, I would like to quote an observation by F. Böckle: "An ever greater number of moral theologians are convinced that moral norms can only be founded teleologically, that is, exclusively by considering the possible and foreseeable consequences of our acts. The main argument of these theologians is that all the goods which are the objects of our acts are exclusively conditioned, created and therefore are limited values".[18]

In quoting Böckle, I would like to point out that we cannot absolutely exclude the possibility of the "intrinsically wrong." Our reflection must therefore be continued by the introduction of another fundamental distinction.

V. THE DISTINCTION BETWEEN "MORAL" AND "PREMORAL" EVILS AND THE MORAL "INTRINSIC EVIL"

In recent years, discussion on "intrinsic evil" has referred to the distinction between "moral" and "premoral" evils (*mala moralia* and *mala praemoralia*).[19]

Moral evils—contrary to "morally good"—are those which, if freely realized, make the human being (as a whole) morally bad. These evils therefore refer to the moral quality of the person, his moral goodness, and are in this sense "intrinsically evil." Examples of such moral evils are, as already mentioned, the readiness to be unjust, unchaste, and unfaithful; also blasphemy, or seducing a person to a sin (that is, to a moral evil). These moral evils which are evils in themselves do not indicate which concrete acts in this world would be a violation of, let us say, justice and chastity; that is, they do not indicate which concrete acts are not morally right and which acts should be realized if a person is to be morally good. But from the beginning of this chapter, I have pointed out that the current discussion on the theory of "intrinsic evil" refers not to personal moral goodness but rather to the material, moral rightness of our activity. The moral rightness or wrongness of our acts has to do not with moral goods and evils, but rather with premoral goods and evils.

Premoral evil[20] does not refer immediately to the moral goodness of a person, but rather to the well-being of human beings[21] in the different areas of human reality. Such evils are, for example, illness, death, underdevelopment, depression, cultural deprivation, etc.—in short, anything in the earthly, human areas that in one way or another is opposed to the well-being and development of the human being. Human beings who are affected by such evils are not therefore morally evil. But a morally good person has to avoid, as far as possible, premoral evils; his purpose is rather to create premoral goods and values for the well-being of human beings. He who, without proportionate reasons, introduces premoral evils into human reality, is acting wrongly. To determine which acts are humanly right, and therefore morally right and not wrong, the consideration of premoral evils is morally relevant: therefore these nonmoral evils are premoral evils.[22]

Although the moral goodness of a person and the moral rightness of his acts should, per se, coincide, this is not in fact always the case. Perhaps someone makes a great contribution to the well-being of humankind but is only motivated in his activity by egotism—for instance, in order to be honored. He has done the morally *right* thing, for he has created premoral human goods or values; but he is not morally *good*. It is evident that there is a relationship between a premorally wrong act and a morally bad act; this relationship has to be considered.

The distinction between moral and premoral evil, on the one hand, and the demand of moral goodness, on the other hand, that we avoid premoral evil as far as possible and act morally rightly, introduces the question: under what conditions is the realization of premoral evils morally wrong, and is it possible to determine "intrinsic wrongness" in this way?

The morally right act in our human world is therefore clearly understood as the realization of premoral goods or values. How can sexuality, mass media, atomic power, etc., serve the well-being of man—man viewed in his innerworldly and inter-personal reality?[23] The problem is in dealing with the horizontal, innerworldly, humanly and interpersonally right and morally responsible self-realization of human beings. The problem becomes more difficult if one considers that man is very limited in his actions in this world: he cannot realize premoral human goods or values without realizing premoral human evils at the same time and in the same act. Cultural values require the nonrealization of certain other human goods or values, accumulation of riches can cause poverty to others, the potentially high values of celibate life condition the nonrealization of the high values of married life (and vice versa), etc. The nonrealization of human goods and values is a premoral evil for human beings. How can we determine, under these conditions, the moral rightness of human acts?

Under these circumstances, moral theologians today maintain that no premoral good —and therefore no good except the divine and the (personal) moral good—is an absolute good for human beings. In the same way, no premoral evil is an absolute evil—that is, an evil that must be avoided absolutely. This also pertains to the human value "human life." In the past we used to call the value "human life" the highest of all human values; today we do not repeat this formula, not even in official Church documents. We call human life the "fundamental" good—but by no means an absolute good. This statement has its consequences.

The realization of an innerworldly and therefore premoral evil would not constitute an "intrinsic evil" because it is not an absolute evil. To put it positively: because of the coexistence of premoral goods and premoral evils in every human act, we must determine the moral rightness or wrongness of an act by considering all goods and evils in an act and evaluating whether the evil or the good for human beings is prevalent in the act, considering in this evaluation the hierarchy of values involved and the pressing character of certain values in the concrete.

Therefore, the realization of premoral evils could be justified only because of the prevalence of premoral goods as opposed to premoral evils. As to the so-called deontologically founded "intrinsic evil," it would be impossible to find a priori any premoral evil that could justify the judgment "in itself wrong."[24] Only if it were possible to show that there is a premoral evil whose realization could never be justified by any premoral good, even if it were the highest and most urgent premoral good, would it be possible to speak of "intrinsically wrong." Deontologically founded "intrinsic evils" would be, per se, nothing but abstractions of the highest level, which presuppose implicit knowledge, at least of all the historically possible combinations of premoral goods and evils.[25] This abstraction of the highest level could only be avoided if it were possible to indicate all the elements in an act (that is judged as "intrinsically wrong") that are relevant for its moral rightness, and exclude all other relevant elements. This is the case in a concretely realized act, and also in formulating a moral norm in which all other morally relevant elements are excluded (for instance, killing someone only for the purpose of pleasing a third person).

The foregoing considerations indicate a problem that is not so simple: how is it possible to determine the proportionately sufficient reasons—as we used to say—that would justify the realization of premoral human evils in realizing premoral human goods? This problem has recently been explicitly discussed among moral theologians in both Europe and North America, in both a theoretical and a casuistic way.[26]

The question is: how is it possible to make a comparative evaluation of goods and evils of different categories (for instance, life-richness-culture-"quality of life")? But this problem is not new in moral theology, and therefore there is no special need to explain it here. For traditional moral theology was also aware of it, and said that determination of the proportionate reason is possible (for example, in judging an act with a double effect, or in decision-making according to the order of charity). We will encounter great difficulties, but these difficulties do not make the task impossible.

Contemporary moral theologians are well aware[27] that in accepting deontologically founded "intrinsic evils," we would greatly limit the necessity for proportional evaluations so that the difficulties of moral theology would, to a certain degree, be avoided and we would finally have much greater security in making concrete moral judgments. But the same moral theologians are of the opinion that these advantages would be too high a price to pay because, first, we would increase the lack of moral objectivity of moral judgments and, second, similar judgments could demand too much from Christians in the concrete realization of their lives.

The defenders of these positions are aware and agree that in our human self-realization the premoral goods or evils are assumed to be on the level of morality, so that they somehow have the character of morality and of an absolute. But there is a contrary opinion[28] which states: premoral evils or premoral goods may most certainly be in a relationship of competition, because they are only relative values and disvalues which in principle cannot demand, per se, to be preferred to other values. But this opinion then holds that because our personal self-realization is a moral activity, these values and disvalues must be considered as moral and therefore absolute values and disvalues. It denies the possibility of a competitive relationship between moral values and disvalues, so that it is not possible to conduct any comparative evaluation as to the hierarchy or urgency of similar values. We may assume that this opinion considers the disvalues of masturbation and contraception in their concrete realization as moral and therefore absolute, so that they cannot enter into a competitive relationship with other values. But one could remark that this opinion forgets one important point: that according to this opinion the other premoral values/disvalues of the acts will also be assumed on the level of moral self-realization and that they therefore would become moral and absolute values that cannot enter a competitive relationship. There seems to be an "atomistic" understanding behind this opinion, for if someone accepts that premoral values enter the level of morality and become moral values, they enter this level of morality not as separate values or disvalues but rather with their competitive relationship. Now, in this case, only the prevalent and therefore relative value or disvalue will become a moral absolute on the moral level! On the level of morality one must not overlook the relative importance of premoral values or disvalues as proponents of these reflections on "intrinsic evil" would insist. A couple considering the various premoral values regarding their marital activity do not find a plurality of moral duties and consequently no moral conflict of duties; they find a plurality of nonmoral values/disvalues, but not an a priori obligation to one or another premoral value, because these premoral values are relative values. Rather there exists only one moral and therefore absolute duty—the duty to the value in the concrete which is the prevalent premoral value. I know that the above example is disputed, but it shows the general problem very well.[29]

VI. THE RESULT OF THE "RECENT" REFLECTIONS ON "INTRINSIC EVIL"

What now is the result that today's moral theologians think they have obtained from their discussion on "intrinsic evil"?

First, the "norms" which have to do with personal moral goodness are not the object of discussion of these moral theologians, for these "norms" undoubtedly establish an "intrinsic evil" contrary to moral goodness. This is true with regard to our relationship to God (the Absolute). This is also true with regard to the values of personal morality and goodness (an absolute). The object of our intention must always be the good and the right with regard to both the general tendency of the person and to the particular area: we are never allowed to be unjust, unchaste, etc. We are never allowed to seduce someone to a moral evil, sin. The discussion on "intrinsic evil" has as its object only the human and moral rightness of the realization of innerworldly and interpersonal and therefore relative goods and values or evils and disvalues.

Second, in the area of the morally right, prohibitive moral norms which forbid an act because it causes a premoral evil would not necessarily always indicate an "intrinsic wrong." This would also pertain to those normative propositions which some authors, because of a deontological way of arguing, suppose indicate an "intrinsic evil." More often one would consider propositions as "prima facie duties," as a certain Anglo-Saxon ethics would say—and Thomas Aquinas said that these propositions *valent ut in pluribus,* are valid "generally." These propositions would therefore indicate a premoral evil that must be avoided as much as is reasonably possible if one wants to act rightly. Such formulations must consider all possible combinations of premoral goods and evils if they are really to indicate an "intrinsic evil." But it is unlikely that they would indicate an "intrinsic evil" that is valid under all circumstances.

Third, normative formulations pertaining to morally wrong acts that would indicate an unquestionable "intrinsic evil," would apply to those acts whose content is completely determined— excluding all other possible morally relevant elements regarding the object, circumstances, consequences, and ends. This is undoubtedly the case in a negative judgment on the moral rightness of a concretely realized act. Such a judgment, supposing it is right, is necessarily universal, that is, in substantially equal situations we should have to judge equally in a negative sense: a concrete "morally wrong" means "intrinsically evil." We should have to judge in the same way if a negative normative proposition could indicate exactly all the possible relevant elements, for instance, in the formulation "it is morally wrong to kill someone merely for the purpose of giving another person pleasure."

Is it all right to venture a flight to the moon? Given the situation of injustice with regard to the distribution of goods in this world or in a particular country, is it all right to be a businessman without first eliminating the situation of injustice? Is it all right to use violence to eliminate unjust violence? Can it be all right for a couple or a nation to follow a policy of contraceptive birth control? Who has to give, to whom, and how much has he to give of his private property in order to eliminate injustice and poverty from this world?

Of course, we can try to answer such moral questions, but not without difficulties. In any case, giving an answer presupposes a sufficient knowledge of all relevant elements of a situation, in order to come to a balanced and well-founded judgment on the moral rightness or wrongness of a specific course of action. Moral theology has always recognized this; it has therefore not tried to answer such questions generally with the aprioristic designation "intrinsic evil." But it has acted differently with regard to certain areas of human reality, for instance, with regard to the good of human life, to marriage, and to human sexuality.

Official Church pronouncements have clearly taken for granted the moral reflections of Christian specialists in ethics. Moral theologians today are concerned with greater objectivity as opposed to abstract and therefore insufficient moral judgments; they are becoming more cautious and skeptical. They introduce their concerns into the discussion of Christian moral theology. They give more attention to general theoretical reflections than to individual illustrative examples and solutions. These authors consider observations like those outlined above as very important for truly objective moral normativeness. If corrections and improvements in moral knowledge occurred in past centuries, why should they not occur in our own time and in the future?[30]

NOTES

1. J. Murtagh, *Intrinsic Evil: An Examination of This Concept and Its Place in Current Discussions on Absolute Moral Norms* (excerpts from dissertation, Pontifical Gregorian University), Rome (1973).

2. J. Murtagh, *Intrinsic Evil*, loc. cit., 17.

3. For example, A. Vermeersch, *Theologiae Moralis Principia-Responsa-Consilia*, Vol. I: *Theologia Moralis Fundamentalis*, Rome[4] (1947), n. 100; A. Lanza, *Theologia Moralis, I: Theologia Moralis Fundamentalis*, Rome (1949), n. 140, I.

4. Thus, J. Murtagh, *Intrinsic Evil*, loc. cit., 29 ff.

5. Cf. B. Schüller, "Neuere Beiträge zum Thema Begründung sittlicher Normen," in: J. Pfammater and F. Furger (eds.), *Theologische Berichte* 4, Zürich (1974), 109–81, on pp. 122–27; F. Scholz, *Wege, Umwege und Auswege der Moraltheologie. Ein Plädoyer für begründete Ausnahmen*, Munich (1976), 40–60.

6. J. Coventry, "Christian Conscience," *The Heythrop Journal* 7 (1966), 145–60.

7. P. Knauer, "The Hermeneutic Function of the Principle of Double Effect," in: C.E. Curran and R.A. McCormick (eds.), *Readings in Moral Theology No. 1: Moral Norms and Catholic Tradition*, New York, Ramsay, Toronto (1979), 1–39; cf. more recently, "Fundamentalethik: Teleologische/als deontologische Normenbegründung," *Theol. Phil.* 55 (1980), 321–60.

8. W. van der Marck, *Liebe und Fruchtbarkeit. Aktuelle Fragen der Geburtenregelung*, Freiburg i. Br. (1964), 37–60; idem, *Grundzüge einer christlichen Ethik*, Düsseldorf (1967), 54–72.

9. E. Schillebeeckx, "The Magisterium and the World of Politics," *Concilium* 6, n. 4 (1968), 12–21; here pp. 14–19.

10. B. Schüller, *Die Begründung sittlicher Urteile. Typen ethischer Argumentation in der katholischen Moraltheologie*, Düsseldorf (1973), 102–11 (² 1980, 133–41); idem, "Neuere Beiträge . . . ", loc. cit., 155–61; cf. idem, "Various Types of Grounding for Ethical Norms," in: *Readings in Moral Theology No. 1*, loc. cit., 184–98. Cf. more recently, "La moralité des moyens: La relation de moyen à fin dans une éthique normative de caractère téléologique," *Rech. Sc. Rel.* 68 (1980), 205–24.

11. B. Schüller, "Neuere Beiträge . . . ", loc. cit., 177.

12. Cf. F. Böckle, "Glaube und Handeln," *Concilium* 12 (1976), 641–47, on p. 645; idem, *Fundamental Moral Theology*, Dublin (1980), 308.

13. On the following observation, cf. E. Chiavacci, *Teologia Morale I*, Assisi (1976), 226; idem, "La fondazione della norma morale nella riflessione teologica contemporanea," *Riv. di Teol. Morale* 10 (1978), 9–38, on pp. 16–18; J. Fuchs, *Responsabilità personale e norma morale. Analisi e prospettive di ricerca*, a cura di S. Privitera, Bologna (1978), 143f; idem, *Sussidi 1980 per lo studio della Teologia morale fondamentale* (for students' private use), Pontifical Gregorian University, Rome (1980), 295.

14. For example, B. Schüller, "Neuere Beiträge . . . ", loc. cit., 115f; J. Fuchs, *Responsabilità personale . . .* , loc. cit., 378f; idem, "The 'Sin of the World' and Normative Morality": *Gregorianum* 61 (1980), 51–76, on pp. 68f; idem, *Sussidi . . .* , loc. cit., 295.

15. Cf. B. Schüller, *Die Begründung sittlicher Urteile*, loc. cit., 164–213 (² 1980, 171–263); idem, "Neuere Beiträge . . . ", loc. cit., 140–53; cf. L. Janssens, "Norms and Priorities in a Love Ethics," *Louvain Studies* 9 (1977), 207–38, on pp. 233–36; J. Fuchs, "I trapianti e l'esperimentazione umana," *Medicina e morale* 2 (1969), 161–81, on pp. 162–69.

16. B. Schüller, "Various Types . . . ", loc. cit., 649.

17. B. Schüller, "Neuere Beiträge . . . ," loc. cit., 122, 141, 148, 153. Cf. Thomas Aquinas, *S.C.G.* 3, 122: "Non enim Deus a nobis offenditur nisi ex eo quod contra nostrum bonum agimus."

18. F. Böckle, "Glaube und Handeln," loc. cit., 644.

19. About this distinction cf. B. Schüller, *Die Begründung sittlicher Urteile,* loc. cit., 102–11 (² 1980, 133–41); idem, "Neuere Beiträge . . . ," loc. cit., 154 f; G. Sala, "Die Entwicklung vernünftiger menschlicher Einsichten," *Concilium* 12 (1976), 634–40, on p. 634; F. Böckle, "Glaube und Handeln", loc. cit., 643; L. Janssens, "Ontic Evil and Moral Evil," *Louvain Studies* 4 (1972), 115–56.

20. Also called *Mala physica* (physical evils: Scholastics), nonmoral evils (Schüller), ontic evils (Janssens).

21. Cf. the already cited text of Thomas Aquinas, *S.C.G.* 3, 122.

22. So, for example, P. Knauer, J. Fuchs, R.A. McCormick, L. Janssens, etc.

23. See again the cited text of Aquinas.

24. Cf. Part IV of this chapter.

25. Cf. K. Demmer, *Sittlich Handeln aus Verstehen,* Düsseldorf (1980), 95f.

26. Cf. P. Knauer, "The Hermeneutic Function," loc. cit.; B. Schüller, *Die Begründung sittlicher Urteile,* loc. cit.; R.A. McCormick and P. Ramsey (eds.), *Doing Evil to Achieve Good: Moral Choice in Conflict Situations,* Chicago (1978).

27. Cf. Part IV of this chapter.

28. C. Caffarra, "Il disordine morale della contraccezione," in: A. Zimmermann, F. Guy, D. Tettamanzi (eds.), *La coppia, l'amore, la vita,* Milan (1980), 299–314.

29. This is the example discussed in C. Caffara's cited article.

30. Some further comments: What is the relationship of this tendency in moral theology to the theories of a certain other tradition in moral theology and to the teaching of other moral theologians?

1) The distinction between moral and premoral evils was not present in the tradition of moral theology in the same way as it is today, but it was not unknown. Look, for instance, at the well-known difference between an act regarded in its physical specification and an act regarded in its moral specification. The same is to be said about the distinction in the Middle Ages between the *malum in se* (e.g., killing) and *malum secundum se* (e.g., murder) (cf. O. Lottin *Psychologie et morale aux XIIe et XIIIe siècles,* t. II, Gembloux (1948), 421–65; idem, *Morale fondamentale,* Tournai (1954), 280f; T.G. Belmans, "La spécification de l'agir humain par son sujet chez Saint Thomas d'Aquin," *Divinitas* 33 (1979), 7–61; J.F. Dedek, "Intrinsically Evil Acts: An Historical Study of the Mind of St. Thomas," *The Thomist* 43 (1979), 385–417).

We find the same orientation in several manuals of moral theology: that sometimes an act that is judged as morally wrong in most cases could occasionally become a morally right act, given special circumstances (for instance, killing because of a proportionally important and therefore justifying reason, e.g., in the case of self-defense when faced with unjust aggression).

2) Today some theologians would prefer to consider what we have called premoral evils always as moral evils (for example, killing, using violence, falsehood), even in a case when causing these evils could be justified. According to these moral theologians, the realization of a minor moral evil would be justified, in a case of necessity, by avoiding the realization of a major moral evil. (E.g., W. Korff, *Kernenergie und Moraltheologie. Der Beitrag der theologischen Ethik zur Frage allgemeiner Kriterien ethischer Entscheidungsprozesse,* Frankfurt a.M. (1979), 77, 86, 88f, 93; A. Auer, "Die Unverfügbarkeit des Lebens und das Recht auf den natürlichen Tod," in: A. Auer, H. Menzel, A. Eser (eds.), *Zwischen Heilsauftrag und Sterbehilfe,* Köln (1977), 1–52, on p. 48.) They observe that such a necessary causing of moral evils does not call for penance and conversion, but rather for regret. It can be presumed that this last observation attempts to indicate that here "moral" has to be understood rather in an analogous sense (cf. M.V. Attard, *Compromise in Morality* (dissertation, Pont. Gregorian University), Rome (1976); H. Windisch, *Handeln in Geschichte. Ein katholischer Beitrag zum Problem des sittlichen Kompromisses,* Frankfurt (1981).

3) This opinion of some moral theologians apparently accepts the possibility of an objective conflict between incompatible moral normative propositions. The aforementioned recent reflections by present-day moral theologians understand that there is a compromise in every (synthetic) action and in every (synthetic) judgment on moral rightness, but they accept such a compromise not as a moral compromise, in the strict sense, but rather as a compromise in the area of premoral and therefore relative goods and values or evils and disvalues.

4) In order to resolve many difficulties in situations of moral conflict, the moral theology of past centuries gave attention to the principle of the act with a double effect and to the distinction between direct and indirect causing of evils. Contemporary moral theologians think that such principles can be replaced by the above-mentioned reflections on the determination of morally wrong acts, with one exception, that of causing moral evil (sin) by seduction ("scandalum"). (Cf. B. Schüller, "The Direct/Indirect Distinctions in Morals," in: C.E. Curran and R.A. McCormick (eds.), *Readings in Moral Theology No. 1: Moral Norms and Catholic Tradition,* New York, Ramsay, Toronto (1979), 215–43; F. Scholz, *Wege, Umwege und Auswege,* loc. cit.; R.A. McCormick and P. Ramsay, *Doing Evil . . . ,* loc. cit.).

5) What is the relationship of the above-mentioned reflections to the well-known teaching on the so-called "only material sins"? Sin was called "formal" if realized with sufficient knowledge and freedom; otherwise, it was called "only material sin." But this distinction of the past between formal and material sin is not as clear as the distinction we

make today between personal evil and material wrongness. For this very reason it is sometimes said that the concept of "only material sin" is an absurdity because sin is precisely a personal evil.

Some moral theologians today prefer to make the following distinction: in the area of personal goodness—that is, of formal morality—the agent's concrete moral judgment is not only subjectively but also objectively the norm. They think that the concept of material sin refers not to the area of personal goodness, but rather to the concept of material wrongness; the judgment of "material sin" would objectively, therefore, not be the immediate norm for moral goodness. It is true that the objective norms of moral goodness—that is, the judgment of the agent and the objective norm of material rightness—would, per se, coincide. Therefore they were often in the past considered—but less conveniently—the objective norm of moral goodness.

According to these considerations, it would also be possible to distinguish between an objectively materially wrong act ("material sin," which is equal to unjustified causing of premoral evils) and objectively personally wrong acts ("formal sin," that is, moral evil). The avoidance of both kinds of wrong acts is the responsibility of human beings, but avoidance is possible only in different ways.

6. Nature and Culture in Bioethics

I. INTRODUCTION: THE NATURE OF MAN— IMAGE OF GOD

About fifteen years ago, the theologian K. Rahner published some brief but fundamental reflections on the theme: "Nature and culture in bioethics." The title of the article was: "Theological reflection on the self-manipulation of man."[1] For Rahner, it is decisive that man is not a "numinous" being (i.e., in a certain sense divine), but finite, created and therefore fundamentally different from a divinity. Such a distinction carries with it the possible justification of a human intervention both in "his" world—what is different from himself—and by his "world"—what he himself is. Man is therefore a being "capable of operating" (Rahner), open to active development and to transformations, although, despite the manipulation, he is and continues to be *man*, in the sense that this "capacity of operating" must not become arbitrary, unreasonable, or inhuman, but must rather demonstrate the conception of man and of his world as "already themselves" and, despite this, "not yet themselves". Such a Christian self-understanding could be of interest also to ethicians of a secular arena.

Rahner's reflections go back to the well-known thesis of the Protestant theologian, F. Gogarten,[2] whose secularizing (not secularist) ethics, developed after the Second World War, has struck a responsive chord with Catholic theologians too. According to Gogarten, the biblical Judaeo-Christian faith has destroyed the numinous and taboo-forming conception of man and of the human world, i.e., of "nature." Such a destruction of the taboo puts man, and his world, back into his own hands so that he may develop it actively and "creatively," to make it ever more itself. This possibility of man does not exclude the possibility of misunderstandings or abuses, or, to put it in other words, the possibility that man may "dehumanize" or even destroy himself and his world. Ethics demands a truly human development, and forbids dehumanization. Distinguishing between the two possibilities, Gogarten appeals to the being/nature of man and of his world.

The theses of Rahner and Gogarten are in line with the biblical thesis of man as the image of God, often interpreted in the sense that it belongs to man to dominate the subhuman creation. Recent studies, in light of the Bible's priestly document, would prefer to speak of the commission to take created reality into one's own hands, to govern it.[3] Such a commission would not permit any arbitrary domination of any kind whatever over animals. This concept goes with the idea that creation "as image" has as its goal the creation of man as "God's partner"—differently from the creation of subhuman reality.[4] On the basis of this idea, man as God's partner would have the commission of continuing the work of creation precisely in the sense of being God's partner, i.e., in accordance with the being/nature of the creature.

Such theological reflections on man and his world suggest the following questions: what are man and his world, and what can they be or must they become in the hands of man—and this, precisely in accordance with nature, i.e., the being of created reality oriented toward its ulterior realization and development? In other words, in what sense is the nature of man (with his world) a nature that is the *measure* for man's action, the norm of activity? As a matter of fact, man understands himself (with his world) as given/gift, and hence as commission; before the creator God, he as partner is responsible for correct development or for possible abuse. In concrete terms, what does this mean?

This brief introduction suffices to make it clear that there are various concepts of nature. In the reflections that follow it will be very important to sort out these various concepts of nature, which are profoundly relevant to bioethics. Here, two distinct concepts of nature emerge: (1) What is the being/nature of particular human realities, e.g. life, ovulation, sperm, genes, chromosomes, etc., that is to say, what are these realities, how do they develop, how do they function, what natural finalities can be distinguished in them, i.e., finalities in relationships with other realities and with man as a whole? (2) What is the being/nature of these realities as gifts/givens and commissions in relation to man as such? The connection between them is that it is a part of the being/nature of created reality, as it is presented to us, to be gifts/givens and to be commissions. Here, then, is our first reflection on this question.

II. THE NATURE OF BEING A PERSON AND THE PERSONAL NATURE

A double terminology is used here in order to indicate that a distinction must be made between the various concepts of nature, if one wishes to determine the nature of man. Man, experienced as gift and as commission, is a person. That is, he "is in himself," as conscious of himself, deciding about himself, disposing of himself, summoned. It is precisely here that the need for distinctions arises: on the one hand, man's nature is to be a person and to dispose of himself as such, as a total unity. On the other hand, his nature is to be a person in all that is of the person, i.e., that which is personal but cannot be called "person" as such (e.g., his intelligence and his liberty with regard to the varieties of human realities, the fact that he is a person and an interpersonal subject among many men, the fact that he is his body and his sexual being, his relationship with other persons and with the various realities of the created world); so that man, as person, must control, at least to some extent, the personal realities which, as such, do not solely constitute the person.

Man's self-realization, therefore—his commission—must develop in both aspects of what it is to be man. On one side, man must realize himself in accordance with the nature of his being as person: self-realization of the person as person—i.e., accepting himself as given/gift and also as commission to complete this self-realization of his manifold personal reality in accordance with the nature of such realities. This self-realization in accordance with (the nature of) being a person is today often called the moral goodness of the person; while the realization of the manifold personal realities in accordance with the particularities of their nature which is given to us (life, sexuality, interpersonal relationships, etc.) is called the moral rightness of the action of the person in the field of innerworldly realities: for these too represent a given/gift and a commission.

The distinction set out here between the two different fields of nature in the whole context of man's being/nature means that bioethics is fundamentally concerned with the area of the nature of manifold human (and thus personal) realities, and that it does not deal directly with the nature of being a person as such.

III. MAN AS PERSON AND MAN AS NATURE

It follows from the foregoing distinction that when we now speak of man as nature, we mean that nature of man which does not coincide with the nature of being a person as such. We find as a "given" the nature of the various realities of man's own being and of the being of his world. But this act of "finding" the nature of natural realities does not take place in a pure encounter, so to speak, at a distance and without the active intervention of the subject which proposes to understand the nature of the realities. When we encounter the realities of our being men, this nature is always already in some sense interpreted; indeed, it is always already—according to our "interpretation"—"assumed" by us, i.e., we have already fitted it into our total reality, and in this sense "transformed" it, in the sense of our interpretation. In other words, when we deal with nature, it has become in some sense, because of our action, a cultural fact.

In fact, man's personal commission, as image of God, is a cultural commission in relationship to the given nature. We cannot assume our human reality without making it a cultural reality. Indeed, it is our permanent commission to continue the cultural activity until now carried out in relationship to nature. This continuous activity demands of us an unfailing will to understand and interpret the nature which has already been understood and interpreted before; it always demands a further cultural transformation of the natural reality which has already been culturally transformed (and thus the transformation of the "nature" contained in the cultural fact already realized). Cultural development obviously does not mean simply preserving what is already there but rather conserving it by means of an active transformation. In this sense, it contains our active intervention upon the natural realities, and in this sense a human artifact. Cultural reality is always nature and "artifact" together—but only if the "artifact" is in line with the given nature as human nature; that is why this is never understood solely as the nature of the particular reality, purely as such, e.g., the human ovum, but in the full sense of the nature of the concrete reality, i.e., as an element of the whole context of the total personal reality "man." If a human intervention in nature is not carried out in the sense of the nature (understood in the sense set out above), it becomes an "artifact" contrary to this nature and is no longer cultural, but an inhuman intervention, a destruction. Thus, for example, are genetics cultural or destruction, when employed for therapy, for improvement, for eugenic reasons?

Bioethics, therefore, is a cultural work only if it is a "nonarbitrary creativity" of man in the vast area of human *bios*. Although it goes beyond the given nature, it takes its measure from this. In what sense?

IV. HUMAN NATURE AND HUMAN REASON AS MEASURE

Culture is possible only if man takes into account both his given nature, distinct from human reason, as an element of measure, and human reason itself, which likewise is a given of nature as an element of measure. Now it is a fact that nature speaks to us of many things, while remaining silent about others, e.g., morals. Reason, on the other hand, can speak a word which becomes for us a moral standard of measure, but in order to do this it absolutely must listen to the word of nature.

The word of nature speaks to us always and only about facts. It speaks to us about man as a personal, interpersonal, historical being. Scientists (doctors and biologists) try to make nature speak about itself. In their study of nature, they see what it can tell us about being: about the nature of genes and chromosomes, about their behavior and reactions in determined circumstances and in particular human interventions. They listen to what it tells us about the laws of nature in the area of the psyche, of social life, and of the fundamental biological adaptation of man's animal nature. They grasp what it says about the probable behavior of human partners, if an undesired or foreign life intrudes into their own sphere of life. They understand what it says about probable personal reactions concerning behavior that is not accepted by the personal conscience. They are instructed about possible or probable behavior in the milieu of the family, of a group, of society, etc., when confronted with certain events. In summary, yes, nature does indeed speak to us, but only about facts, about what is, and about what will happen, perhaps or probably or certainly, under specific conditions in the sphere of human realities, thus giving bioethics pieces of information about what is, happens, or will happen in the vast sphere of the *bios*.

But when questions that are, properly speaking, moral arise for bioethics—i.e., questions about what can or must be done morally in the sphere of the *bios*—nature is silent. The measuring standard is no longer simply nature, but reason, informed by nature about the facts. Reason is the measure to tell us what we can or must do morally vis-à-vis nature's statement about the facts, inasmuch as reason perceives, evaluates, and judges the natural reality which informs us about itself, in that it is the nature of man—whether such a process of reasoning occurs as explicit reflection or as an act of intuition (though never without "reasons"). This information, which acts as a moral measure born of reason, is immediately taken up by the "moral experience," or conscience, i.e., by moral obligation.

We have already seen that reason, as the measuring standard in questions of moral obligation, must reflect, of necessity, on the information given to us by nature; and it is not only a case of a nature that is observable with relative ease—for example, in the sphere of human sexuality—because nature gives information about other less "readable" realities too—for example, about psychological and social elements in the development of marriage, of the family, of political society, etc., and about the reality of technical and economic processes, on various phases of the growth of human life, and so on. Man's reason, thus informed, must reflect and attempt to distinguish, for example, what one can or must undertake responsibly, as man, in the field of technology or economics; how one can or must treat life, responsibly, in its various phases of development, both with regard to life itself and with regard to other human beings rightly interested in it, and to society; to what extent one can or must, responsibly, promote certain activities and scientific research under determined social conditions, etc. Nature, as distinct from reason, therefore, does not give us information about such moral problems, and thus the solutions are not to be "read" in nature alone. Man must seek the adequate response, reasoning, evaluating, and judging, in reflection on himself as person and then on the data of the information provided by nature, which includes both the relations of particular realities with other particular realities and their relationship to man as a whole, in his concrete situation.

A traditional formula says that what is to be done "is read in the nature of things"; obviously, this formula must be approached very cautiously. It will be extremely difficult in certain areas to say how "the nature of things" in themselves can be the measure of responsible moral action, precisely because nature gives only information; this is true also of those areas in which it often used to be thought relatively easy to discern what was morally appropriate action, e.g., the area of sexuality. Actually, a strenuous investigation is necessary in these areas no less than in others, taking into account the vast fields of the effects and diverse values, as well as the various phases of physical development, in order to understand what can be a humanly appropriate action.

When man attempts to make a reasonable evaluation, i.e., under the moral aspect, he also pays attention to the fact that although he does know the nature of human realities, he knows it only imperfectly and rather as the nucleus of many variations, the product partly of natural causes and partly of human inter-pretations and interventions. For this reason, one can say precisely that nature is a totality composed of the nucleus and its variations.

There is certainly awareness that, as a creature of culture, man can arrive at a better knowledge of nature even through attempts of dubious morality; in certain cases, there may also arise the question of the licitness or not of "daring" particular attempts of dubious righteousness, whose aim, looking to a greater knowledge of nature, would be to open up new ways to a kind of action or behavior that would be of great help to humanity. To put it briefly: *culture*, in its moral dimension, is established by reason, distinct from nature but informed by it. Precisely because reason reflects not only on the particular realities given us by nature but also on their existence within the whole reality of personal and interpersonal man (this reality too being given to us), man has within himself the capacity to evaluate and judge which interventions for transforming the particular natural realities are justified or even necessary. Such behavior corresponds to man's being/nature as such.[5]

V. NATURE, REASON, FAITH

One can and must speak of nature in the foregoing way if one wishes to define the concept of nature clearly and truthfully. It is also true, however, that the various concepts of nature mentioned hitherto are always already assumed in a yet higher and vaster concept of "nature": man, in fact, exists as one called by God, in Christ, and—as a Christian—as a believer. The final element of his being/nature consists in this. This being/nature contains in itself all that we have hitherto called the being/nature of man and is generally meant by these terms. A detailed, lengthy discussion of this point would go beyond the aim of this essay; we limit ourselves therefore to a few brief pointers.

First: what has just been said about the being/nature of man allows us to understand what is the final horizon, the final meaning, and the deepest dimension of human existence, of man's self-understanding, of human self-realization and action. This horizon, this meaning and dimension, permeate every moral norm and judgment, and likewise every human decision and act—though without being explicitly spelled out. Faith, which establishes and takes up this horizon and norm, is the point of departure for the Christian's self-understanding, for his search for and identification of moral norms and judgments, and for his decision-making and action in the human world.

Second: Christian faith, inasmuch as it is *fides rationem illuminans* or *lux evangelii* (*Gaudium et spes*), is a light in the search for and identification of good and right behavior. But as a light, it aids in seeking and identifying moral norms and judgments, without, however, giving these itself. To this light also belong the examples and orientations of revelation with their instructive character and importance for a decision and action worthy of man. But, here again, the *fides illuminans* does not replace reason.

Third: faith as *fides quae* can also lead us to make decisions in moral matters that are in fact right and good; indeed, it can lead us to decisions that are a *proprium christianum*, e.g., to celibacy for the kingdom of God. But even in such cases, it is always human reason—illuminated, to be sure—that justifies such decisions.

Thus, the broad concept of the being/nature of man contains every other true concept of human being/nature. It does not replace these concepts, but confirms them and prevents them from becoming hypostatizing concepts of human nature. Therefore, even the Sermon on the Mount does not replace them, but it does make up for the defects of the moral concepts of its time.

NOTES

1. In: K. Rahner, *Schriften zur Theologie* VIII, 260–85.
2. F. Gogarten, *Verhängnis und Hoffnung der Neuzeit,* Stuttgart (1958); cf. J. Vohn, *Sittliche Erkenntnis zwischen Rationalität und Glaube. Ein Aspekt der Säkularisierung im Licht der Theologie F. Gogartens,* Paderborn (1977).

3. Cf. N. Lohfink, " 'Macht euch die Erde untertan'?", *Orientierung* 38 (1974), 137–42; cf. idem, "Die Priesterschrift und die Grenzen des Wachstums," *Stimmen der Zeit* 192 (1974), 435–50.

4. Cf. C. Westermann, *Creation*, Philadelphia (1974), 55–88.

5. On this whole essay, cf. J. Splett, " 'Macht euch die Erde untertan'? Zur ethisch-religiösen Begrenzung technischen Zugriffs", *Theol. Phil.* 57 (1982), 260–74.

7. Human Authority—between the Sacral and the Secular

Unless one grasps that man's personhood is essentially interpersonal and societal, it is impossible to discern what is morally correct behavior in man's world: only with such an understanding is it possible to avoid a one-sidedly individualistic ethic. The interpersonal and societal reality of man is necessarily bound into particular structures and institutions, and this link produces the phenomenon of authority in relationships among men. The question arises, for ethics and moral theology, as to what such authority is understood to be; for what such authority establishes conditions the correct behavior of man in his world, and thus the content of the moral and absolute "thou shalt."

Man's fundamental way of looking at things conditions his answer to the question of what such human authority is understood to be. The answer of the (agnostic or atheist) secularist will be different from that of the moral philosopher who has a theology of creation; but even the reply of the latter will take on different nuances of a theology of revelation, according to whether he thinks as a Muslim or a Jew or a Christian—and there are differences even among different Christian denominations. In what follows, the Catholic understanding will be reflected upon, as distinct from the secularist, but the Catholic understanding too has proposed schemas with different nuances. Since some of these appear primarily sacral while the schema which appears profane or secularizing (the opposite of sacral) corresponds best to a theology of creation, the title of this chapter explains our purpose: "Human authority—between the sacral and the secular."

The authority of the state (with its subdivisions such as regional and local authority) will serve in what follows as the type of human authority. But it must be pointed out here that there exists analogously a varied authority in other institutions and groups: in marriage and family, in the relationship of parents and child, in freely chosen institutions (e.g., in the undertaking of common work, in a school), in free groupings (e.g., in youth groups), etc. Human authority exists in the Church too, especially in the hierarchy. Inasmuch as special problems can arise here, these must be dealt with in particular, if only briefly.[1]

I. HUMAN AUTHORITY—SEEN FROM THE PERSPECTIVE OF THE THEOLOGY OF CREATION

The perspective on human authority of the theology of creation is fundamentally different from every secularist (agnostic or atheist) understanding of the ethics of correct behavior in the formation of the human world.[2]

1. For the secularist understanding of the ethics of the construction of the world, the phenomenon of human authority presents basically no special problem. Where human authority shows itself to be necessary, it will be taken into consideration in the particular understanding of ethics, like every other human necessity and fact in this world; the question of how human authority can justify absolute moral requirements is thereby no particular problem in the sum of ethical requirements.

2. This is not so in an understanding of man and his world from the perspective of the theology of creation. This is sufficiently clear from the various kinds of attempted solutions to the problem which have existed in the history of ethics and moral theology, and still exist today. How can human authority be the basis of absolute moral ties and commitments—of an entire juridical order with its innumerable concrete consequences? What is the role here (other than in any secularist understanding) of God, who alone is absolute and justifies absolute requirements? The various kinds of attempted solutions are conditioned in each case by different understandings of the world of man as creation.

The most sacral of the attempted solutions is conditioned by an utterly unsatisfactory concept of creation, according to which it is not possible to posit within the realm of created human reality the authority to establish absolute requirements such that these bind the personal man in his conscience and thus before

God. In the reality of creation, only the executive authority (= the moral justification) to establish appropriate or necessary ordinances in the concrete societal situation is recognized: this alone is authority in created reality. It is not, however, understood as authority in the sense that moral commitments in the personal conscience arise from its ordinances as such. Only God himself, in this understanding, can be the source of such a tie, God who as the transcendent absolute encounters the particular person directly in his conscience and binds him to follow the ordinances of human authority. Thus the creator supplements what is lacking to creation as such. In this view of things, one does not see in what sense the created reality itself is a created participation in the reality of God, which is absolutely transcendent and precisely for that reason most deeply immanent in creation.

This view of things corresponds in a certain manner to the view—in another realm of human reality—which concludes, from the fact that God is the only absolute Lord of every human life, that men do not have disposition over human life except where God himself permits this. In this view too, which even today is set forth in important official documents, creation is understood as something that lacks an essential element for its self-realization: the transcendent God himself has disposition directly over human life (and in this, there is never a clear solution to the problem of how the creator God reserves to himself such disposition or transmits it to us). The fact is that God is the transcendent Lord of life, not a Lord within this world—and not only Lord of life, but in the same manner Lord of every created reality.[3]

The view which we have set forth is correct in saying that an absolute in this world ultimately presupposes the transcendent absolute; its attempts to clarify how the transcendent absolute presupposed by the created reality has effect in the created world must, however, be considered unsuccessful. Indubitably, this sacral interpretation of the phenomenon of human authority offers scarcely any starting-point for a possible dialogue with men who think in a secularist perspective. This is not so in the interpretation which makes use of the concepts of participation and representation in its understanding of human authority.

3.   This other interpretation understands human authority as the representative (*vicaria*) of divine authority; its basis is a

fuller and deeper concept of creation. According to this understanding, human authority itself participates in God's authority. The authority of God (itself) is present in the human authority (itself). This needs no supplement through the transcendent absolute, whose authority is at bottom immanent in the human authority. A few years ago, a well-known philosopher wrote that human reason (*ratio*) is the "vicar" of the transcendent absolute—in the understanding of moral obligation in the conscience too.[4] This applies equally, then, to the understanding of such an obligation on the basis of the necessity of human authority. In this sense, despite the positivistic overtones of the formulation "to institute," one may read also the words of the Apostle Paul: " . . . there is no authority of the state that does not come from God; every authority is instituted by God. Therefore whoever opposes the authority of the state, opposes the ordinance of God . . . Therefore it is necessary to obey, not only out of fear of punishment, but above all for the sake of conscience . . . they act as commissioned by God . . . "[5]

It is perhaps easiest to understand human authority as God's representative if we presuppose an absolute ruler and his authority. This is fundamentally the same, even when it is effected and effective through an oligarchy or a democracy, and with a varied distribution of functions. Differences of opinion in ethics and moral theology in past epochs—which are acute even today—are more easily understood against the background of the experience of the human authority of an absolute ruler. But there are essentially two different interpretations of the "representation of God."

One of the two chief interpretations of the representation of divine authority in human authority originally sees the representative as a physical person: as God's representative, the person who bears the authority has a sacral character. Hence it was above all to the physical person who embodied the authority that the character of "coming from the grace of God" was attributed. On the basis of this sacral character of the ruling person, his action too was brought into closest proximity to the working of God himself, as we shall go on to show. A decided voluntarism (which undeniably has its historical origin in nominalism) in the understanding of the activity and ordinances of human authority, thus understood, corresponds to this.

Another interpretation, noticeably less sacral, is not so much concerned with the person in the understanding of human authority. Here, it is not so much the person as such, who has the authority and therefore can act authoritatively, who is the central concern, but more importantly it is the *function* of this person in society, in the service of this society, and made necessary by the society itself. Thus the person is more servant than lord; he must carry out the required function and is thereby implicitly the servant of the creator. The personal man, his societal character, the necessity of social institutions, the necessity of authority as leadership and power: all this is the creative work of God. Insofar as that society, God's work, essentially needs authority, authority leads society to its required and desirable functioning, and is established in creation itself as execution, realization and continuation of creation itself. The one who carries out this function—precisely because he carries it out, and inasmuch as he carries it out—has the corresponding authority, in the representation of God. Hence it is not because someone has attained authority that he can make ordinances, but rather the other way round: inasmuch as someone has to carry out the function of authority, he has also the corresponding authority. Thus, the one-sidedly sacral character of the person who bears the authority disappears. (We should particularly note that in this understanding, authority exists only for an act that is a function in the service of the correctly understood good of society and of its members; this is clear also in the text cited from the Letter of the Apostle of the Gentiles to the Romans.)

If human authority is understood as the representation of God above all in the sense of a commission to serve, as the continuation of the work of creation through the ages, and not primarily in the sense of lordship (with the highest ruler, God), then it is more easily comprehensible in a democratic society. The attribute "representation" and "coming from the grace of God" applies also to authority and power, as these are variously distributed in democracy. Only, we must bear in mind what these formulations ultimately intend. One will have recourse much less than in the past (or in the ecclesiastical present) to the will of the lawgiver when problems arise (what is this will, in a parliament where various motives determine the voting?); rather, one will look to the legislation and the law itself; we shall come back to this point. When the individual ruler retires, this is not so much because he had received a personal "investiture" for a limited period ("Please be our ruler for the time being"), but rather because his commission expires with the expiring of a function of service in society. This is how democracy is to be understood.

An example may clarify what has been said. The father of a family is both head of the family ("authority" in a certain measure) and educating father of his son ("authority" in a certain measure). Gradually, the son grows out of the father's educative task, and so the father "loses" authority. But if the son remains in the family community, he remains still, in the appropriate manner, under the "authority" of the head of the family.

II. PERSONAL AND FUNCTIONAL UNDERSTANDING OF HUMAN AUTHORITY—CONCRETELY UNDERSTOOD

Both the personal and functional interpretations of the representative character of human authority, understood from the perspective of the theology of creation, necessarily have their consequences for the understanding and ethical evaluation of concrete phenomena of human authority. Concrete examples have been thoroughly considered in the philosophical-theological discussion over the course of centuries, and have significance even today in a changed situation and with partially new terminologies and ways of thinking. A few examples will now demonstrate the acute relevance of both perspectives on human authority, and their consequences.

1. A first problem is that of dictatorship. This is understood here as a rule by force which substantially and viewed as a whole works against the good of the society over which it presides, instead of serving it. Here a first problem, that of legitimacy, presents itself. As the history of ethics shows, whoever attributes human authority (in divine representation) above all to the person, runs the risk of identifying legitimacy and legality, so that circumstances could arise in which the legitimacy of dictatorship would be recognized, solely because the dictators came to power by legal means. Against this, one who fundamentally makes legitimacy dependent on the nature and finality of human society and of the function which serves this finality, will in such circumstances deny the legitimacy of the one who in fact bears power, not only because of a lack of legality, but also and above all because his exercise of power is substantially hostile to the society. Even under the dictatorship of National Socialism, some Germans were willing to judge the question of legitimacy only, or at least primarily, on the basis of the question of juridical legality ("assumption of power"). It is deficient legitimation that decides the question of whether the rulers who lack such legitimacy may justifiably be removed, even by violent means, and replaced by legitimate rulers, or by rulers historically legitimated by their actual installation in power (this is how I should wish to understand it); this would presuppose that this could be attempted, avoiding still greater damage to the society than the already existing damage. For this reason, many have seen as justified the attempt to change rulers in Nazi Germany by violent means, without taking into consideration the question of legality, both at the time and especially afterward. The last decades have shown that the question posed here about the basis for understanding human authority has ever fresh relevance in various regions of this world.

But the second question too is continually relevant: how should one understand the authority of dictatorial rulers, as long as power does actually remain in their hands? Viewed from the perspective of creation theology, is this a case of genuine authority which therefore participates in God's authority, and in which this divine authority ultimately is present? Is this an authority which the members of the state must "obey" because it is the "representative of God"? We know from the history of ethics and jurisprudence up to very recent times that those who uphold a more personal understanding of the representation of God through human authority deny genuine authority ("representation of God") to the illegitimate possessor of power. Accordingly, they deny any genuine obligation of obedience to a superior whose authority they do not acknowledge as genuine; the only obligation which they acknowledge for the people of the state is the obligation to carry out the necessary ordinances which the de facto ruler issues for the corporate life of the state.

These considerations are consistent in themselves, but they have a very nominalistic ring to them: a duty to carry out ordinances without any obligation of obedience. We do not find this nominalistic-sounding formulation in the other understanding of (God-given) authority, which answers the question of legitimacy, like the question of authority, on the basis of the *function* within the society. If the authority is attributed not primarily to persons but to functions, then the execution of this function, as an activity instituted for the society by the creator God, cannot lack the corresponding authority. There is an authority which is illegitimate and yet genuine; for the moment, it is not prevented from replacing the legitimate authority with an illegitimate authority, and is, in this sense, a genuine authority.

One is obliged in conscience to obey even this illegitimate but genuine authority, where it exercises real authority, i.e., when it issues ordinances for the correctly understood good of the whole body. It would probably be possible to find even modern jurists who would understand this second conception of authority.

2.   A second example of the twofold interpretation of the concept of human authority, on the basis of the theology of creation, as a participation in divine authority, would be what has been discussed for centuries in ethics and law as *epikeia* in relation to authoritative ordinance and especially to law. While human authority finds its genuine basis in the historical development of human society, nevertheless both authority and its ordinances lack the possibility of achieving ultimate concreteness. It is impossible ever fully to encompass this concreteness, whether through the formulation of atemporal legal decrees or through historically authoritative legislation and cultivation of law; even the latter cannot ultimately do full justice to the concrete reality of the society and of its members. This is true above all because the concrete reality exists in continuous historical development. What in Plato and Aristotle, and later in the philosophy, theology, and canon law of the Christian Middle Ages, up to very recent times, was and is called *epikeia* seeks to do justice to the "deficient situation" in human society which has been described: with all respect for a formulated order of creation and likewise for justified authoritative legislation, *in concreto* circumstances arise in which a solution which is not covered by the literal formulation of ordinances is recognized as the only just and correct solution.

This problem is certainly seen and discussed in modern jurisprudence also; for example, "hermeneutics in law"[7] is one of the modern ways of thought and formulations which in its own way—at least partially—deals with the problem of *epikeia*. The same is done by the other formulation of the problem: whether circumstances arise in which it becomes necessary to reflect on the "deeper" and "more general" sense of given laws, or on the contemporary tendencies which implicitly manifest themselves in the process of legislation and the establishment of law.

In the question of *epikeia* too, the significant difference of the double interpretation of human authority as participation in divine authority is seen. The personal interpretation clearly shows its voluntaristic character here: in the situation of conflict, one has recourse (*epikeia*) to the will of the authority (thought of, above all, as a physical person), not to the will which has already been manifested in the given legislation, but to the presumed present will of the bearer of authority, who must be addressed as such even in a situation of conflict; the authority, like God's will which governs all things, is thought of as "benevolent." *Epikeia* is thus defined as a restrictive interpretation of the law in accordance with the presumed benevolent will of the authority. It is not easy to see how such a situation of conflict under given laws in a parliamentary democracy can be meaningfully understood. One point remains correct, at any rate: the reflection on the tendencies of contemporary authorities and on the attitude that is authoritative today can serve as an indication for the correct understanding of authoritative ordinances; even some contemporary jurists would agree with this.

The functional understanding of human authority as "God's vicar" understands *epikeia* differently. According to this interpretation, *epikeia* seeks nothing else than simply the correct solution of the case of conflict which is under the law and its societal function. The point of reference is not a presumed will of a continuously directing (benevolent) ruler, but the law that has already been issued authoritatively for the good of the society. *Epikeia*, therefore, is concerned with nothing other than the correct application of the law even in the case of conflict, which has not been explicitly covered in words by the law, but is dealt with in the deeper and more general meaning of the law—hermeneutics. For this reason Thomas Aquinas calls *epikeia*, not a restrictive act of interpretation of the law, but the virtue of better justice—better than the virtue of mere obedience to the words.[8] This too is welcome to many jurists today.

3.   A third example of the difference between the personal and functional understandings of the presence of divine authority in human authority concerns the division of moral and legal ordinance in the case of penal laws. The human legislator in most cases threatens punishment if what he prescribes is not observed; but not always. For example, many Christian politicians in Italy, in the discussion of a new penal law ordinance on abortion, were concerned above all that every abortion should be declared by the law to be a crime, even if in particular individual cases one might refrain from punishing the crime. The same perspective is

found in the declaration issued on this question at that time (1973) by the Vatican Congregation for the Doctrine of the Faith.

In the opposite direction, so to speak, another theory asks whether there cannot exist "pure" penal laws, i.e., laws that carry with them no necessary moral obligation in conscience and yet threaten punishment if they are not observed; examples that come to mind are tax laws, traffic ordinances, and all ordinances which, if not carried out, impose so-called administrative penalties. This theory has existed since the Middle Ages, and (in dependence especially on F. Suárez) is strongly upheld in Catholic moral theology even today, to the astonishment of many jurists. Its justification presupposes the typically personal understanding of the representation of God by human authority, granted that the lawgiver has the will to gain the observation of certain ordinances exclusively through threat of punishment, and not through moral obligation in conscience; he could indeed bind in conscience also, but does not will to do so. Here the sacral understanding of human authority goes so far that it makes not only the ordinance of society directly dependent on the will of the lawgiver, but, equally directly, the moral obligation or lack of obligation in conscience; it follows that the human authority would formally decide on moral obligations. Against this, it must be objected that the representation of God does not go so far, for human authority does not have this necessity, and therefore does not have this justification. (One should note how different this kind of sacralism is from the other, which, as mentioned above, deduces the moral obligation of human ordinances directly from God, and does not see this as mediated in any way.)

In any case, the theory of "pure" penal laws is losing adherents today. At its base lies a mistaken understanding of human authority, for this is not to be understood personally, but functionally: God's authority, which of course must be understood as the final and transcendental justification of moral obligation, is active, imposing moral obligation, directly in human legislation, and human authority itself cannot be directly in charge of moral obligation as such through decisions of its own will. Rather, the moral obligation which comes from divine authority is mediated through the human authoritative ordinance of the corporate body. God's authority is present as participation in human authority; the latter therefore cannot simply free one, through a decision of the will, from the moral aspect of an ordinance. Thus, human authority is neither morally irrelevant nor simply directly dispository in the realm of the moral; it is the mediation of divine authority.

Such a liberation from unfounded sacralism could awaken fears of a certain rigorism. Is every dot of legal ordinance a question of conscience? Such an anxiety is without foundation, for human authority and legal order are at the service of the good of the society and of its members. It belongs to this good, however, not only that human laws are just, but also that the manner of their application be reasonable for men, e.g., in the areas mentioned above. Here, therefore, one must bear in mind what was said in the last example about *epikeia* as the correct—and thus, humanly reasonable—application of laws.

This means, however, that tensions can arise in society. It is possible that the executive organs of authority cannot recognize what seems to us a justified situation of *epikeia*, and therefore impose a penalty—that is, a penalty without (moral) guilt. Presumably, this is a case of penalty only in an analogous sense, i.e., something imposed for the maintenance of good order, something that as such can be justified and must be accepted.[10]

III. CIVIL AND ECCLESIAL AUTHORITY

Hitherto, we have considered human authority above all in the type of the authority of the state. This was done, however, in the awareness that authority exists in many other ways in human society, with analogous problems, as indeed in that human coming-together we call the Church. Ecclesial authority is therefore also a kind of human authority which mediates divine authority, but has its own character, which justifies a short treatment on its own.

1. The divine authority mediated in civil authority appears explicitly to so small a degree that the Christian and the agnostic can find a large measure of agreement about it. The divine authority which is mediated only "civilly" is therefore basically known about by the Christian, but little reflected upon (so that there is an easy temptation to disregard it).[11] Against this, the ecclesial authority, although human, is much more strongly felt by active Christians to be sacral and "divine." What is the reason for this? Clearly, not because it mediates divine authority in just the same way as the civil authority—rather, because the good that authority establishes in the ecclesial society is of a special kind. For it is the good of a society that owes its existence not only to a human necessity, but to a positive act of foundation in Jesus Christ; it is the good of a society that understands itself as a society of salvation, and hence a different good from that to which the civil authority is committed. This means that a divine authority of a particular kind is present and mediated in human (ecclesial) authority. The special sacrality of ecclesial authority is felt, not because it too is human authority, but inasmuch as it is concerned with a particular realm of reality of the divine care for man.

What has just been said is concerned first with the area of ecclesial authority—compare the new Code of Canon Law— which is active in guiding and leading the Church's society in the realm of the goods that belong to its salvation. One can distinguish from this the authority which deals with saving truth: it too is human authority mediated from God, but its certainty comes from the assistance of the Holy Spirit. The realm of that power (authority) which is to be considered as sacramental could give the impression, however, that it is not so readily to be categorized like this. Certainly, there are analogies here; but fundamentally, the power to posit sacramental acts is also a human authority that is given by God and represents and mediates divine authority. The fact that in many cases it requires particular sacral rites for its bestowal is only a question of the manner of the bestowal of such authority, which anyway rests on a positive act of establishment.

In the realm of ecclesial authority, therefore, Christians should see the special sacrality of its sphere of activity, but at the same time they should see its character as a functional human authority, which participates in divine authority and mediates this, in just the same way as the civil authority. On the other hand, Christians should also see in the functional civil authority the participation in divine authority and the mediation of this— even when they can come to a meaningful agreement with the agnostic about this authority, leaving out of account its deeper dignity.

2. Yet one more word must be said about this realm of civil authority, for it too does not exist wholly outside the reality which ecclesial authority serves directly.[12] In a certain analogy, therefore, civil authority shares in the dignity of ecclesial

authority. If, because of the divine will to save, there is no reality having absolutely nothing to do with the kingdom of God that has dawned in Christ, then this is true also of human communities and of the authorities that serve their good. Whatever good they do, ultimately looks to the reality that has dawned in Christ; and this reality is served even when—in the case of politicians or fathers of families, etc.—what is done is done as a mere matter of fact, perhaps with a mentality that is agnostic or wholly secular.

In what has been said, one thing should be understandable: the divine authority and claim are mediated to us even in realities which we, justifiably desacralizing and secularizing, call profane. Because they know this, Christians distinguish themselves from their agnostic-secularist contemporaries, but can work with them in a common will to construct the profane world by laying bare necessities, requirements, and moral obligations, which ultimately imply a claim that is made (though it is generally not understood explicitly as such) by the creator God and by him whom he has sent.

NOTES

1. This essay is a complete revision of an essay published twenty years ago: "Auctoritas Dei in auctoritate civili," *Periodica de re mor., can., lit.* 52 (1963), 3–18.

2. On the questions dealt with here and below, one may compare: J. Fellermeier, "Autorität," in: *Lex. f. Theol. u. Kirche* 1 (1957), 1132–35. M. Zalba, *Theologiae moralis compendium* I, Madrid (1958), nos. 306–8; 538–42; 447–57; 1341f. and 1590,4. M. Reding, *Philosophische Grundlegung der katholischen Moraltheologie* (Handbuch der Moraltheologie I), Munich (1953), 112–24.

3. On this, cf. B. Schüller, *Die Begründung sittlicher Urteile, Typen ethischer Argumentation in der Moraltheologie,* 2nd ed., Düsseldorf (1980), 236–51.

4. J. de Finance, "Autonomie et théonomie," *Gregorianum* 56 (1975), 207–35, at 230f.

5. Rom. 13: 1–6.

6. On this, cf.: F. Suárez, *De legibus* lib. 1, c. 5, n. 24, with *Actas del IV cent. de Suárez* II, 197–209, 243–67; E. Jombart, in: *Nouv. Rev. Théol.* 59 (1932), 34–44; E. Romero, *La concepción suareziana de la ley,* Seville (1944).

7. Cf. A. Kaufmann, "Gedanken zu einer ontologischen Grundlegung der juristischen Hermeneutik," in: N. Horn (ed.), *Europäisches*

Rechtsdenken in Geschichte und Gegenwart (Festschrift für Helmut Coing z. 70. Geburtstag), Munich (1982), 537–48.

8. Thomas Aquinas, *S. Th.* II-II, q. 120, a. 2, ad 1 and 2.

9. 18 November 1974.

10. This is also a reply to a query of J. Giers, "Epikie und Sittlichkeit," in: R. Hauser and F. Scholz (eds.), *Der Mensch unter Gottes Anruf und Ordnung (Festgabe Th. Müncker)*, Düsseldorf (1958), 65 (no. 77).

11. The 1960 Roman Synod believed it must act explicitly against such a mentality among the clergy.

12. On this, cf. H.U. von Balthasar, "Nine Theses in Christian Ethics," in: C.E. Curran and R.A. McCormick (eds.), *Readings in Moral Theology, No. 2*, Ramsey, N.J. (1980), 190–206.

8. Faith, Ethics and Law

The following pages are addressed to lawyers engaged in a debate concerning the problem of "natural law today."[1] I have not used the term "natural law" in the title. Today many theologians and philosophers, including myself, prefer to speak of the "humanum" and of "human rights" instead of "natural law." This change in terminology helps us to avoid several misunderstandings. Besides, the use of these words also adds accents and nuances which throw more light on the problem of natural law and enrich its understanding.

Those who think that natural law, whether we use this term or not, is an important category, insist that it is not possible to consider true rights to be only those which are protected and enforceable by law ("*ius quia iussum*"). I am of the same opinion. The main problems are: (1) To have rights which are protected and enforceable by laws it is necessary to assume a right to establish those laws and rights. Such a basic right cannot be a positively stated right. (2) Because there is a plurality of rights (and of principles of law), a positive order of rights necessarily supposes that some rights (and principles of law) already exist independently of positively stated rights.

What has been said about the two basic problems of natural "rights" will be softened a bit if we bear in mind the fact that "rights" is an analogical concept, that is, a term which is not always used in the same sense. Much depends on the definition of "rights" that one assumes. Nevertheless, we can say that these two basic problems mentioned above (and many other problems depending on them) suggest the problem of the "absolute" in morality and law.

Formulating in this way, I am not yet speaking on the topic "God," at least not explicitly, because the question of the absolute is also seen in a nontheological sense in law and in ethics.

Nevertheless, because I am dealing with the topic "natural law," as a moral theologian (that is, in theological ethics), I prefer to begin precisely with the concept of the Absolute, in the sense of the God who communicates himself to us in Jesus Christ.

It is well known that the term "natural law" has been used in the past, and is used today, very often equally in both the areas of law and rights and of morality. To a certain degree I shall do the same in the present reflection; nevertheless, we will distinguish explicitly between the field of law and rights and the field of morality. But as a moral theologian, I prefer to start in the area of morality, thinking that the problems here may throw light on the problems in the area of law and rights.

The content of our reflection will fall into three parts: (1) the importance of an "absolute", both for morality and for rights, (2) "natural law" as moral order, (3) "natural law" as an order of rights (and principles of law).

I. THE IMPORTANCE OF THE "ABSOLUTE" FOR MORALITY AND FOR RIGHTS AND LAW

Addressing the topic of morality and rights means speaking of realities that have "binding force." Morality means moral judgments, moral norms, moral principles, while "rights" means various rights as well as principles of law. When we speak of binding force, if the term has a true meaning, we mean something "absolute." Here we are dealing with the most complex problems in the areas of morality and rights.

It is certainly possible to avoid the question of the absolute, that is, the question of a binding force, by considering it "agnostically" as a question without solution. For the object of the problem of the absolute is not merely the pragmatic and functional meaning of particular orders of morality and rights, but rather their absolute meaning based on a true meaning of man as such.

It would also be conceivable that one could try to reduce the many particular rights to some rather basic ones. But this approach would be an impossible attempt at a *regressus in infinitum*. The real question is whether or not orders of morality and rights which seem to make sense in themselves and in the here and now can be understood as expressions of the whole of "being human" that reveals itself, not as meaningless, but rather as meaningful and absolute.

The absolute meaning of "being human" seems to be the condition of possibility of morality and rights. Without this meaningfulness, it is, in the end, senseless to talk about the binding force of orders of rights and morality. It is quite an interesting phenomenon that so many philosophers of law and ethics who call themselves agnostics (with regard to the meaning of the "whole" of "being human") wholeheartedly devote their entire lives to problems of rights and morality. The same can be said about the phenomenon that millions recognize a true binding force of rights and morality (in whatever way this may be). It would seem that behind the talking about and "living out" of the binding force of rights and morality is to be found a nonreflected consciousness of the meaning and absolute binding force of the "whole" of "being human."

Several theologians (for example, B. Lonergan, K. Rahner, K. Demmer) have reflected on these questions along the lines of transcendental philosophy and theology; they believe they must answer this question positively. The same questions and answers seem to be implicit in the observations of those who today express their conviction about man's ultimate and immediate basic confidence in the meaningfulness and absoluteness of the innermost human reality, and this confidence is asserted even though they do not directly answer the very difficult theoretical question about the absolute meaning of the human being.

May I suggest another parallel: a few years ago, one of my students was writing a doctoral dissertation on the ethics of the Dutch Humanist Association. These humanists explicitly declare themselves agnostics, but they are especially interested in ethics and therefore work ecumenically with Catholics, Protestants, and ecumenical groups. They recognize that morality and rights imply an "absolute," and this not only in the sense of a functional pragmatism. Insofar as they, as agnostics, are not able to give this absolute the name "God," in a traditional sense, they call it *mysterium.*

A similar observation was made some years ago by the well-known sociologist and philosopher M. Horkheimer, who insisted that we have an absolute need of "theology"; this does not mean that he (who was an agnostic) had found faith in God, the traditional object of theology, but rather that the meaningless injustice in this world cannot be the final word on humanity. Looking at this and similar observations, my question is again to what degree are these different formulations of the recognized binding force of rights and morality not implicitly felt and lived as an expression of an "absolute" binding force?

I would like to point to another fact. For several decades there has been in Poland an interesting tendency to try to understand the phenomenon of morality and rights philosophically. This tendency originated with some humanist philosophers (T. Gzeżowski, T. Kotarbiński), but was also taken up afterward by a number of Catholics (Karol Wojtyla being one of them) and by some Marxist ethicists (M. Fritzhand). This rather mixed group of philosophers, which has today been joined by other ethicists in the West, is convinced that the phenomenon of morality, that is, the absolute "ought" (and therefore also the absolute character of "rights"), is an absolute and irreducible (cognitive) basic experience of mature man. The value of this experience is just as basic as our original understanding of the first theoretical logical principles. The absolute binding force, in the sense of the basic moral experience, transcends particular moral and juridical binding norms and thus makes them into binding absolutes. Clearly, the basic consensus of these ethicists does not prejudice the question of how one goes about reflecting explicitly about the possibility and nature of this so-called basic experience, and also how an abstract order of morality and rights can be given content.

Theologically, and therefore among theistic religions, the absoluteness and absolute binding force of moral and juridical norms present themselves in a different way. For example, the basic concept of Judaism, at least as some understand it, sees the God of the Covenant as the positive source of rights and duties. This understanding may be still stronger in the fundamental concept of the will of Allah in a theistic, Islamic religion. It is clear that similar theistic concepts have a tendency to eliminate what we should call natural law. Nevertheless, I would also like to put the question whether in this sort of understanding, the natural law problem may not be implicitly present—that is, how can one be reasonably and morally justified in accepting these absolute binding norms of the God of the Covenant and of Allah?

Christian theology sees the problem of the absolutely binding force of rights and morality in a different way. This does not exclude the fact that many theologically less well-informed Christians see the foundation of absolutely binding norms almost solely in the "will of God," who has positively decided in this sense; therefore, their understanding would not be very far from a certain Judaic or Islamic concept. But within Christian theology, too, there are different tendencies, and we can see quite different emphases and nuances spelled out by several theologians. Here the main question is to what degree does faith assume or imply reason and to what degree does reason, which understands human morality and human rights, imply the light of revelation? In other words, in what way do faith and reason support one another? Basically, we can say: Christian faith acknowledges and recognizes man, his nature, his being a person, his reason, as the creation of God. It understands that humanity, freed from its sinful alienation from God through Jesus Christ, is accepted by the God of Love. God belongs to the specificity of man, whose ultimate dignity thus stems from God. God does not give positive rights and duties to man; rather, man is the image of God and participates therefore in God's providence.[2] Humanity therefore must try to discover by itself an order of rights and morality for man and society in this world. The binding force of the order of rights and morality, found in this way, is absolute because it is founded in the reality of man himself, created by God and redeemed in Jesus Christ. The content of such an order of rights and morality will be determined by what is found to be good for man himself.[3]

What has been said is not in opposition to the doctrine of Vatican II[4] that man, who tends to be egotistic, receives God's help always and everywhere, by grace and by the light of the Gospel, so that he can try to discover and reach a human (and thus a natural law) order of rights and morality; the given formulation is important insofar as it says that man receives help, but does not receive the actual content of concrete solutions.

In conclusion, we may say that Christian faith and Christian theology give more evidence than human research alone that the right order of morality and rights ("natural law"), discovered and formulated by man himself, is an order of absolute binding force.

II. "NATURAL LAW" AS MORAL ORDER

Thus, man is bound by an absolutely binding moral order. This does not mean that the moral code of norms has been given to him positively, or has been imposed on him, but rather that he has to live in a true sense as a man, not nonhumanly; and this duty has an absolute binding force. To live and act humanly means proceeding reasonably, not arbitrarily, in an attempt at being—in everything—fully a person in the expression of our human nature. "Human nature" is to be understood here not as an abstract metaphysical concept, but rather as everything that in fact and in the concrete constitutes man in the here and now: therefore what belongs to him either according to the concept "man" or according to what he has become through his historical development, but also everything that he is today concretely, because of his self-formation in society and as an individual. Taking into account this entire reality, man tries to discover as *persona humana* how to realize and to develop further this concrete human reality in a reasonable way.

This understanding of the moral order, discovered by man himself, is the reason for the teaching of a long Christian tradition, that the material content of the norms of human behavior and action of Christians is not distinctively Christian, at least not in principle and *per se*. In other words, the so-called "natural law" in its moral sense means nothing other than the innerworldly way of living by which men express the meaning of their lives, and by which Christians therefore also express their Christian faith (their living relationship to Jesus Christ).

Philosophically speaking, natural law understood in its moral sense means precisely this: that human beings find and experience themselves, concretely and historically, as persons in their human nature. Consequently, this means that man finds and experiences himself while carrying out his task of searching and following, according to the given reality, the way to true self-realization. Theologically speaking, it could be said that man has been set free by God as Creator and Redeemer to a freedom that binds him to strive constantly for a right and better understanding of his reality and of the corresponding way of true self-realization.

What is important in both philosophical and theological speech is that man's first duty is not to fulfill an imposed concrete order, but rather to project and discover such an order of human self-realization. I should like to point out and insist that the term "self-realization" does not mean an egocentric or an egotistical interest, but rather the task of realizing this self in its full individual, interpersonal, and societal self-transcending meaning and openness.

Thus, man has to come closer and closer to "fulfilling" himself. Man is a being of becoming, not a being created in its full development. Man is therefore not simply a given reality that has to be "conserved" as it is, but is a reality that must be developed through personal responsibility. In this sense, we say that the given nature of man must be more and more humanized[5] by man himself. Nature alone is therefore unable to express or indicate personal, moral duties adequately. As already mentioned, nature by itself makes us understand only particular "laws of nature" in the physiological, psychological, etc., sense and the finalities of particular elements of nature. With regard to the given and ever more known particular realities with their particular laws of nature, we must understand and use them by employing our reasoning powers. Moral norms and solutions have to be discovered by observing and reflecting on both the concrete manner in which these elements of nature are in fact realized and the relationship they have to the wholeness of human life. In this sense, we can say that the measure of moral norms and judgments is not directly a given human nature, but rather the equally given human reason.

But human reason is itself measured by the whole of the human being. In accordance with extensive knowledge, experiences, insights, and evaluations, human beings project reasonable ways of behavior and action. They do so (or at least they try to do so) while being both determined and creative. This is not subjectivism but rather the opposite, because in formulating both abstract moral propositions and concrete moral judgments, we observe and respect *all* that is morally relevant, precisely in order to be "objective." This is also the meaning of the traditional scholastic adage which says that the *lex naturalis* (natural law) is *lex indita* or *lex interna* (internal law); in other words, that the natural law is in itself not a written or given code of moral norms but is rather man himself insofar as he can understand and formulate normative moral propositions and judgments in a right way.[6] It is therefore true that our moral norms and judgments, if they are rightly formulated, are true "natural law" and participate in the "eternal law" of God. On the other hand, it is also true that man, as a finite and limited being, can err. It is therefore quite understandable that in the past, many moral formulations were said to be "of natural law," meaning *recta ratio*, although they were in fact not reasonable, not expressions of *recta ratio*, "natural law"; and surely this also happens today. Even grace, the "light of the Gospel,"[7] and the word of the Church cannot totally exclude this possibility.

But something else seems to be more important. Thomas Aquinas observed that man is a changing being.[8] This has consequences in establishing and formulating normative propositions of natural law. This is true, at least inasmuch as these propositions are not only extremely general principles. Extremely general would be such principles as: "always act reasonably," or "do what is good and not what is evil," or "never commit a moral evil, do not perform a nonmoral evil, as far as this is reasonably possible." Similarly, the following formulations would be extremely general: that we should be "human"— "reasonable" in acting in the various areas of human life, for instance, duly distinguishing between my property and yours, between the interests of the individual and those of society. Similar very generally formulated norms and normative propositions are in fact understood immediately and without further reflection, but they do not indicate the more concrete norms of human behavior and action. While concrete moral judgments about the here and now are in themselves "always" right if they are right, concrete moral norms which have been discovered and formulated as universal by man, are not always adequately formulated and right (as explained in the fifth chapter). Perhaps their formulations refer to special societal, economic, or cultural facts, etc. If they do not take account of all possible finalities, consequences, and circumstances, then what they are saying may not be applicable without further distinctions, under conditions that were ignored in their formulation. In fact, it is our duty to try to act according to the truth, according to what is objectively the right thing to do, considering therefore the whole reality of the here and now. Only moral formulations that are truly exclusive, i.e., excluding any other circumstances and finalities other than those mentioned in a norm (for example, "never killing someone merely in order to give pleasure to a third person") are applicable without exception; they are therefore universal in the strict sense of the word. If negative, they indicate an "intrinsically evil" act, as we used to say.

But the question is whether this can also be said with regard to other normative moral propositions, as, for example, "not killing," "not sterilizing," etc. which, as such, do not yet consider all eventually possible circumstances, consequences, and finalities, that is, the whole of a concrete reality. It seems to be right to say that such a "you shall not" can be proved applicable only generally, not universally in the strict sense of the word. Because in order to be really "objective" and "true" in our behavior and action, it would be necessary to consider the moral relevance of the whole concrete reality. If one would like to speak of justified "exceptions" (*epikeia* in the area of morals, not of positive law[9]), this would mean nothing other than reducing the normative moral propositions formulated by man to the precise here and now applicable objective norm.

A final observation is due regarding the so-called natural moral law, or natural law morality. Precisely because natural law morality is not given to us in the form of a code of normative moral propositions, but rather these propositions have to be sought and found by human beings themselves, most moral norms of behavior and action are not metaphysically evident. They are founded on human evaluations which, as such, cannot give metaphysical certitude but only a reasonable, practical, so-called "moral" certitude. The absolute binding force of moral norms and judgments which we discussed above does not suppose insights into these norms and judgments that are metaphysically evident and certain; it refers rather to moral norms and judgments which, in the area of human behavior and action, cannot easily exceed "moral certainty." As long as such propositions, and the insights and evaluations expressed in them, do not change, these normative propositions and judgments, being practically the only ones possible here and now, have an absolute binding force.

We shall have to judge in a similar way in the area of rights and law.

III. "NATURAL LAW" IN THE SENSE OF RIGHTS AND PRINCIPLES OF LAW

There is obviously and undoubtedly a relationship between morality and rights. The so-called golden rule is true without exception: "Do unto others as you would have them do unto you." This formula refers clearly to many different areas of life and behavior, but it has a special application in cases in which we find, in ourselves or in others, not only a justified "expectation," but also "rights" to be respected. "Rights" may mean that we must leave or give to everyone what is his own.

Something is considered as belonging to "you" or to "me," that is, as a right, because it is owed to a human-personal existence and to everything that makes possible the corresponding human development of this existence. In a similar way we can also speak theologically, that is, from the viewpoint of the God of creation and redemption. From the moral viewpoint, the virtue of justice demands first of all respect for what is or has to be acknowledged as one's "due." Therefore it also demands a readiness to collaborate suitably with the order of rights and to foster the security of rights among individuals and in society.

Rights and an order of rights are values which are understood (perhaps without explicit reflection) as objects of what belongs to the "ought" or the "you shall"; those phrases reflect the original cognitive experience as something that is absolutely binding, that is, an absolute. Rights and the order of rights are therefore evaluated as absolutely binding on the basis of an experience and insight we call "moral."

Another question is: what belongs to what we call "rights" (and "just") and to principles of law and order of rights? Those lawyers who accept the idea and reality of "natural law" will answer these questions differently from other lawyers—for example, positivists. If someone has, like me, a starting-point in theology and theological ethics, he must first of all understand, as already mentioned, that the concept of "rights" is an analogous one. If someone states by definition that we can speak of rights in the full sense only if we consider "rights" that are positively protected by law, in society, then we have to understand that he does not necessarily exclude our speaking of "rights" also in a less than full sense, and therefore differently from the given definition. Rights in the full sense of the purported definitions may not include, for instance, the largely recognized "human rights" (at least not all of them), nor a large part of the "international rights" of nations, nor the rights rooted in the so-called natural law.

Nevertheless, one who affirms the reality we call natural law (juridically, philosophically, and theologically) insists that the rights and the order of rights founded in natural law are rights and orders of rights in the strict sense of the word, at least to a certain degree, and that they are basic to the rights which are positively established and protected in society. Even without considering the positively recognized rights of society, I should understand it as an injustice, a violation of existing rights, if someone were to arbitrarily deprive another of his life, of justly obtained goods, of honor and of public reputation. The question here at stake has not only to do with justified expectations, but with rights in the strict sense of the word. Moreover, society and its representatives cannot establish rights—and especially not arbitrarily recognized ones—without violating other rights, unless they are based on previously existing rights. If these preceding or founding rights exist, every statement and recognition of particular rights has to serve those "true rights."

How can we understand what is a formally recognized right in society if it is not justified, and in this sense "unjust"? Is it a true "right", or does it perhaps mean a "right" that is (both juridically and morally) not binding? From the viewpoint of natural law, I would call it "nonright," "injustice." I am sure that not all lawyers would accept my formulation, and I know that my formulation would have practical consequences. On the other hand, we should not forget, in discussing this question, the analogous character of the concept of "rights"; but the formula "nonbinding rights" (I am speaking of concretely specified rights) seems to be senseless.

A further question is: Who knows, and how does he know what are to be considered as a concrete human being's natural "rights"? The above reflection regarding the natural law in the sense of the knowledge of a moral order has to be applied also to natural law in its juridical sense. In fact, during his history and development man (human society) has been able, at least to a certain degree, to "find out," "project," and "discover" what human rights may or should be. Insofar as the natural law in its juridical meaning also brings with it moral obligations, it pertains to the same area as the possibility of moral knowledge. There are, certainly, rather unhistorical and perfectly describable rights and principles for establishing rights, but they are, I suppose, rather rare. More precise formulations have to take into account different cultures, the developments of society, changing evaluations, deeper and developing insights into certain values and corresponding rights. This is so already in the area of so-called commutative justice, where the question deals with "yours" and "mine" in a narrow sense. This is much more important where we have to deal with rights of groups or societies. What are the group's rights with respect to the individual's rights? It is important also where the so-called human rights must be determined more exactly, as well as various rights (and corresponding duties) regarding social justice.

The rights of actual human beings, and the so-called human rights, have essentially an interpersonal and societal character; this is also true when these rights belong to what we call natural law. They are "absolutely binding"; but their applicability is not absolute and unlimited, for they have to be compatible with the rights of others and of society. In what appears to be a conflict situation, the problem of which rights are to be considered as taking precedence, and therefore the only existing rights, has been a real difficulty both in the civil and ecclesiastical areas for centuries. Vatican II's decree on religious freedom, *Dignitatis humanae*, for instance, was not possible before the time of the Second Vatican Council, and it came about only at the end, and not without massive resistance. In apparently difficult cases of conflict, what conditions determine the prevalence of one set of rights? Is it the truth (for example, in religious questions), or is it the personal freedom of conscience and religion? The Vatican Council itself decided in favor of the latter. Here I shall only indicate that there are many parallel questions in law, for instance, that of the conscientious objector to military service or the convinced criminal.

It should be an obvious consequence of our few reflections on natural rights and orders of rights in the sense of "natural law," that natural law itself needs to be positively recognized and stated in society. Thomas Aquinas[10] states that only in this way can the rights of natural law become "efficient"; second, that only in this way can uncertainties about rights in society be ended; and third, that only in this way is it possible to arrive at needed further determinations in various matters which, from the viewpoint of natural law alone, are either not yet determined or are not evident enough. From the viewpoint of natural law, there is a right and duty to ensure the "establishment" of rights in society. Therefore, we must consider positively protected rights and laws, to the degree that they really establish "rights" and not "injustice" as being "absolutely binding."

There is no question that the equal affirmation of the need for natural law and for positively protected rights in society causes problems for both the lawgiver and the judge, and occasionaly also for the citizen who has, for instance, the right to vote. I shall obviously not enter here into the area of casuistry. Basically, I should like to say that there cannot be a "right," a "binding right," for instance, of the state-society, that demands what one considers to be immoral or that imposes itself on freedom of conscience. In this last case, someone could perhaps ask whether, in an extreme case—for example, the case of a convinced criminal—an order of rights could be justified that practically imposes the choice of martyrdom on the "criminal" for what he thinks is the truth.

We must distinguish from juridical obligations the juridical permitting of institutions for the sake of the common weal which juridically leaves it to the citizen to decide whether or not to do something which, according to many, is morally wrong (for instance, divorce).

But the question also concerns the possible opposition between legally protected rights and rights according to natural law. There is, for instance, a defensible right that belongs to those "without rights" to bring about change in "situations of injustice." I am thinking, for example, of certain situations in Latin America: How far is the lawgiver or the government allowed to go along with such a situation of injustice, when too abrupt and turbulent a juridical change would mean perhaps a greater evil, bearing in mind the whole situation? This resembles the above-mentioned question of what may be the prevalent value and rights in given cases of conflict.

Confronted with lawyers and philosophers of law, the theologian is very often interested in the concept of the binding force of morality and rights. From the viewpoint of theology as a reflection on faith, he will offer a special understanding of this concept. He will place this concept in relation to original human insights and experiences, and to philosophical and juridical reflections. What we call an absolute "binding force" he admits in both the area of morals and in the area of rights. In both areas, the binding force, on the one hand, cannot be founded simply in a positive establishment of norms and rights. On the other hand, we can understand and experience in an original and human way both the nature of this absolute binding force and also, though in a different way, the concrete content of what is binding. I have tried to show this first in the area of morality, in order to reflect on it in a parallel way afterward, in the area of law and rights. After all my reflections, I think that, while respecting the analogy of the concept of rights, we have to accept the idea and reality of a true, binding natural law in the sense of natural rights and a natural order of rights. The natural law, on the one hand, will find its full effectiveness only in a positively stated law and in positively protected rights in societies, while on the other hand, the natural law is the deepest value of the positively established order and this is so precisely because the natural law exists *in* the positive law.

NOTES

1. The original text of these pages was conceived in German. The title "Glaube, Sittlichkeit und Recht" is not easily translated into English. While the term "Recht" can mean both "law" and "rights," in these pages sometimes the term "rights," sometimes the term "law," and

sometimes both terms, are used. And while in English the Latin term "lex naturalis—natural law" is preferred, German prefers the Latin term "ius naturale—Naturrecht."

2. Cf. Thomas Aquinas, *S. Th.* I-II, 91, 2c.

3. Thus, Thomas Aquinas, *S.C.G.* 3, 122.

4. *Gaudium et spes*, no. 46.

5. Thus, Vatican II, *Gaudium et spes*, nos. 53 and 55.

6. Cf. Rom. 2, 15.

7. Vatican II, *Gaudium et spes*, no. 46.

8. For instance, *Suppl.* 41, 1 ad 3.

9. Cf. Josef Fuchs, "*Epikeia* Applied to Natural Law?," *Personal Responsibility and Christian Morality*, Georgetown University Press, Washington, D.C. (1983), 185–99.

10. Cf. *Suppl.* 65, 1 ad 2.

PART III

Moral Teachers within the Church

Teaching Morality: The Tension between Bishops and Theologians within the Church

9. Teaching Morality: The Tension between Bishops and Theologians within the Church

It is no secret that a certain tension exists between representatives of the Church's magisterium and representatives of scientific theology. This is indicated not only by occasional single incidents that attract notice, but also and much more by a rich theological literature on the specific theoretical and pastoral problematic. As was the case some decades ago with exegesis, it is moral theology that is today particularly affected. The fact that the American book series "Readings in Moral Theology" has seen fit to dedicate its third extensive yearly volume to the theme "The Magisterium and Morality" (1982), is eloquent.[1] Those who follow the copious "Notes on Moral Theology" which appear each year in the American Jesuit periodical *Theological Studies* will testify that this tension has been mentioned repeatedly in recent years. We are here referring not only to the magisterium of the Bishop of Rome and of his Vatican Congregations, but also to the teaching authority of the bishops in moral questions in general. This essay will deal particularly with the many bishops, scattered in various lands.

Ideally, the activity of bishops and moral theologians ought to display cooperation and a turning to each other for help; certainly, this does exist, yet it is impossible to overlook the tension that today is an extensive and worldwide fact. Bishops show skepticism; they believe that they ought basically to be suspicious about moral theologians—in general, because of the moral-theological method, and in special individual questions.

Moral theologians feel that they are not taken seriously; their experience is that their research, endeavors, and results are met with reserve, and that indeed on occasion doubt arises and is expressed about the purity of their scholarly and ecclesiastical motives. Correspondingly, there is a certain suspicion on the part of moral theologians about the episcopal magisterium, in whose utterances the theological endeavors of moral theologians frequently are either not reflected at all or else, as we have said, are judged skeptically.

In the title of this essay, bishops and moral theologians are named intentionally without the article "the." For not all bishops are meant: there are also bishops who see and take very seriously the problematic of today's moral theology; there are some who say this openly, and some who occasionally admit it "tacitly." In the same way, not all moral theologians are meant: there are also some who are readily heard "above" because they take a skeptical stance before the problematic of today's moral theology and speak indeed from a position of defense, for they do not tackle the problems that arise today in the same way as their colleagues (as is their full right). These are able to give bishops the replies that some of them knew all the time anyway, and would be glad to see confirmed.

From what has been said so far, it follows that this essay speaks not only of bishops in their relationship to moral theologians, but also of a certain group of moral theologians, priests and laypeople, who for one reason or another do not accept their reflections, hypotheses and results of contemporary moral theology. But the primary subject here is the teaching authority of the bishops, which has a particular weight in the Church's moral teaching. Some of what is said here can be applied by analogy to other members of the Church in their relationship to today's moral theology or to certain of its representatives. The chief basic concern of this article, however, is not so much the correct relationship between episcopal magisterium and moral-theological scholarship, as rather concern about a correct Christian ethos and a genuine ethic of Christians' conduct in today's world, an ethic free or set free both from anxieties and from libertinism, i.e., an ethic that seeks to encounter and respond to the great and small problems of every day with judicious objectivity, in the greatest possible independence of the presuppositions of one side or the other. The greatest possible "objectivity"—that is our cue.

I. CHRISTIAN MISSION AND CONCERN

The theologian who speaks on the theme of "bishops and moral theologians" must necessarily begin by reflecting on the mission and corresponding concern of the bishops. For their mission generates corresponding concerns; and these concerns will, or can, easily determine the behavior of the bishops. The theologian who cannot think himself into the situation of the bishops ought not to express himself on this theme. Nevertheless, he cannot avoid recalling his own mission and the concern that is generated from it. We have here different missions and concerns, which, however, serve the same end: that is, they are complementary and supplement one another.

1. The Bishops' Function of Establishing Unity. The Christian ecclesial body is a fellowship of those who follow Christ in freedom, as a fellowship of believers bound together in the Church—hence, as a unity. The bishops are understood and respected as those who maintain and care for unity as bearers of a corresponding mission. The bishops themselves must, and do, understand themselves as bearers of this mission. This self-understanding is the basis of their endeavor and of their care for the community of Christians which understands itself as an ecclesial unity.

It is beyond doubt that the bishops have their particular "function" within the ecclesial community of the believers. They will see their function as one of bearing concern and striving so that the ecclesial community of Christians as such "functions." There exists, however, the danger that they will identify the ideal with an attitude in moral questions that is as free as possible from tension; an attitude that is uncritical, consciously "conformist," not pluralistic, bound to tradition, and remaining aloof from the probing critical questionings of "others"; and that they will encourage a life lived in such an attitude. The use of the word "danger" here does intend to call into question the values of such an attitude; but it could be an attitude that contains an unnecessarily burdensome alignment of one's life, that fundamentally has little to recommend it.

The bishops' function of establishing unity is directed to the faith of the Christian community. The Second Vatican Council speaks explicitly of a faith that must be "applied" in Christian living.[2] Doubtless, Christian (moral) living has to do with faith; but there exists the danger that, for the sake of the unity and immutability of the Christian faith, one would wish to teach and proclaim a unity, uniformity, and immutability, grounded in this faith, of moral directives. Faith indeed has its importance for the establishment of moral modes of behavior, but by itself it does not make this establishing possible. This is what is meant by the teaching on natural law which is based in the Bible and in the Church's tradition. When the Second Vatican Council observes that in some cases even believing Christians with the same degree of conscientiousness can come to different solutions to significant human questions (hence, to moral questions),[3] this shows that the bishops' function of establishing unity in moral questions is not unlimited because of the one faith.

The bishops who are concerned and bear the heavy burden of their responsibility know that they are one part of a greater ecclesial community, and know that they are under obligation to this greater unity. For their teaching about Christian morality in accord with the Christian faith, they will seek the support of Christian tradition, of the teaching of other Christian communities and their bishops, and, in a special measure, of the direction of the Bishop of Rome as a basic foundation stone of Christian unity (and hence also of Christian moral teaching) and of his Vatican Congregations. And this is right, to avoid there being as many Christian communities with their own individual moral teaching as there are diocesan bishops. But even this self-insurance does not take the whole load off the bishops in their function of establishing unity, for these significant supports are not outside history, nor are they realities wholly raised above the process of evaluating and establishing.

If the bishops are concerned with the right functioning of their communities—in moral persuasion and perhaps also in the moral conduct of life—as indeed they must be so concerned, and as far as possible in fellowship with other Christian ecclesial communities scattered through all the world, nevertheless functional unity must not be the chief aim of episcopal concern. If one grasps the difference between Christian faith and moral ordinance (even that of Christians), one will understand that a functioning unity in questions of faith is much more significant than a similarly functioning unity in moral questions. Church history also shows that the functioning unity in moral questions by no means implies the truth of the moral perspective taken up in this unity. In other words, the bishops must be more concerned with moral truth than with peaceful consensus in moral questions. For it can also be the case that moral statements, though widely accepted in a well functioning consensus, nevertheless permit freedoms or impose burdens that have no basis in Christian faith, and do not show themselves over a long period of time to be God's will.

2. The Episcopal Service of Moral Truth.

The episcopal service aims, therefore, not so much at well-functioning unity as at unity in the truth—in the sphere of moral theology too. If more attention had been paid to this in the course of the centuries of the Christian Church, i.e., if *inter alia*, those who called for moral truth had been obeyed rather than the trend toward well-functioning unity, then certain events that we regret today would never have occurred (it is irrelevant whether we choose problems of freedom of conscience and religion, of the defense of unjustified use of force, of concepts in sexual ethics, etc.) This also means that, had one thought more about the question of the truth to be mediated in the case of moral behavioral norms for action in the world, rather than about the mediation of subjective security for the decision-making situations that necessarily arise, then many dramatic instances of conflict would have been avoided.

Naturally, the bishops themselves will feel the possible tension between the requirement that they mediate moral truth and the constantly repeated requirement that they preserve and mediate security for pressing moral decisions. The neo-Scholastic tendencies in theology and in the utterances of the Church's hierarchy—especially before the Second Vatican Council—often served a need for security more than they served the truth and the reasoned establishing of moral decisions. Today there is a frequent lament that this tendency led to an excessively static thinking about natural law, and also to a positivizing of "Christian" moral teaching through frequent interventions of the hierarchical magisterium.[4] If today's theologians—perhaps because they have become more open and more free for essential reflection on the basis of the common work of bishops and theologians at the Second Vatican Council—believe they must point to this factual situation, then the bishops cannot and must not close their eyes to this knowledge; and this allows them to experience the potential dilemma of security/truth in a new and different way.

To this extent, the role of the bishops in the sphere of moral questions is not wholly easy. Moral theologians have experienced a compassionate smile, or a smile that came from a security impervious to doubt, as their reward for being true to their task as theologians by pointing out genuine problems that were not seen elsewhere. Not infrequently, the theologian remains quiet, in order to escape such a smile or further consequences.

Nevertheless, no one should doubt that bishops wish to serve the truth in the sphere of morality. Is this not precisely why they ask the advice of moral theologians? But one must in turn ask, which moral theologians are consulted, or which advice of the various moral theologians is finally accepted? This often depends on the moral theology of the professor who taught the bishops (a few or many years ago) and whose views they now take (all too positivistically understood) as the "teaching of the Church," since they themselves have mostly been hindered from pursuing further studies in moral theology. This is, however, quite understandable; often there lies behind a concrete tension between bishops and moral theologians ultimately nothing other than the tension between different schools of moral theology. In any case, it is the bishop who bears the official service of the unity of the Church's fellowship; this service of the bishops is onerous, because the service of unity should be a service of unity in truth.

The Second Vatican Council draws the attention of all Christians, including bishops and moral theologians, to the fact that the Church is essentially a pilgrim Church, and therefore in constant need of renewal.[5] This is true also to a certain extent of the sphere of moral teaching. This has above all two consequences here: first, life in history, and especially the high speed of today's life, poses new moral problems, which have to be tackled not only by the moral theologians, but also—in relation to the theologians—by the bishops who are called to the service of unity: the solution of worldwide socioethical problems, the responsible use of atomic power, the position to be taken vis-à-vis bioethical problems of a completely new kind, the correct attitude to quite varied kinds of partnerships similar to marriage, etc. The required renewal in the sphere of moral theology implies, second, the recognition that new knowledge can also demand a rethinking of moral solutions of earlier periods, unless one wishes to take the risk of abdicating the effort of finding a greater objectivity than was possible at other periods, because of the wish for a definitive and "certified" possession of a body of knowledge; we shall return to this point. It is a matter of the episcopal service of unity in truth.

We must draw attention to yet another statement of the Second Vatican Council: namely, that we do not always have an immediate and valid solution ready-made in the Church when new ethical problems are posed.[6] Then the expert scholars must be allowed their say, and the (perhaps) disparate attempts at solutions by ethical philosophers and moral theologians must be taken into account, so that finally it may be possible to offer the service, not of an absolute edict or condemnation, but of a careful, very precisely formulated aid that is supported by well thought out reasons. Such statements, which clearly work toward moral truth, are surely a better service of unity than a definitive word that seeks to mediate a supposedly absolute certainty.

3. The Service of the Moral Theologians. In the first Christian centuries,[7] bishops were very often also the theologians of the Church; that is, they not only had the pastoral office of serving Christian unity in truth, but also undertook the theological work of reflection and of deeper understanding. They did this also in some moral questions. Even today, there are bishops who are theologians in the scholarly sense; but this is not normally the case. Theologians, including moral theologians, are today on the whole not bishops. There is no fundamental necessity for a commissioning by the Church in order to be a theologian. But where and when such a commission is given, it is not understood as a "delegation" of the specifically episcopal ministry or of the bishop's teaching authority; recently, Pope John Paul II, quoting Paul VI, explicitly pointed this out.[8]

Since the Council of Trent, but especially in the last century, a strongly juridical understanding of the magisterium as "demanding assent," has become central; this was not so earlier. According to this understanding, the moral theologians' task should be understood primarily and extensively as the scholarly reflection and confirmation of already existing magisterial directives in moral questions. This is how it is expressed above all in Pius XII's encyclical *Humani generis* (1950).[9] Even today, this understanding is widespread although the Second Vatican Council began to shift the emphasis by its reference to the whole People of God as bearer of the Holy Spirit. In other centuries, bishops and theologians mostly looked to the "teaching authority" (above all, the consensus) of the theologians and theological faculties,[10] but now reflection centers rather around the theme of the episcopal office. Moral theologians are aware of this situation, and work and behave accordingly, even though they often know the recognized limits of the authority of magisterial statements and instructions in moral theology. This situation certainly permits an harmonious and fruitful cooperation of the activity of bishops and moral theologians, as a common service of the People of God.

Experience teaches, however, that the situation just outlined contains dangers. One of these dangers is the tendency, already lamented, to a positivism of the magisterium, a tendency to which many believers and moral theologians, but also bishops, succumb. Such a positivism can hinder the research of moral theology, as well as the living process of the establishment of moral truth; this process is never definitely finished. (One should note that such a positivism can also lead to the one-sided granting of privileged status to one moral-theological school above the others). A second danger (easily verified today) is the encouragement of the belief that we encounter God's instructions, made known through positive revelation, in concrete moral directives (e.g., in concrete statements about social ethics, in concrete comments on questions of war and peace, in documents on sexual ethics, etc.). A third danger is that of cramping or narrowing moral-theological reflection. Finally, one should not overlook the fourth danger, that the situation sketched here is apt to promote a permanent "moral immaturity" in the establishment of moral truth (in L. Kohlberg's sense), or the formation of "superegos" (in Freud's sense)—as one may observe in lay-people, priests, moral theologians, and bishops.

Like other theologians, moral theologians too certainly have a particular authority of their own, whether they practice theology with an official commission (e.g., as professors) or not (even though it is true that the commission represents a certain sign of confidence on the part of the episcopal office). Moral theologians know that they are under obligation to the People of God, especially to the moral will of believing Christians. If publicly practiced theology is always implicitly proclamation, then so is publicly enacted reflection of moral theology. For it is the moral theologian's task in the Church to identify the relationships between ethos and moral ordinance with the faith, to undertake the hermeneutic reading of the Bible in the awareness of moral questions, to read hermeneutically the moral traditions (and their history) that have grown up in the course of time, to deepen and develop moral values, to establish moral principles and norms credibly and contextually, to clarify the significance for correct moral behavior of the findings of other sciences, to tackle newly arising moral problems, etc.

These tasks in the realm of moral theology are all the more important, in that the good, and especially the correct moral behavior of Christians to a great extent does not follow directly from the Christian faith, but must be established in a reasonable reflection and evaluation that is enlightened by faith.

Here we see too that the research of moral theologians serves not only the People of God in general, but in a particular way those who must undertake the episcopal service of unity in truth. The task of moral theologians is therefore not only to seek more deeply the reasons for the teaching that has already been laid down by the magisterium, but also to prepare such a teaching and to make it possible. Responsible episcopal directives cannot be drawn up without a serious listening to what serious moral theology has to say. How often does one hear that the bishops are challenged to make a clear statement on particular significant moral questions. But do they always already possess the responsible answer that is demanded of them?

But what if some bishops do not trust "the moral theologians"? What if it seems to them that the moral theologians sow "confusion" in the People of God? Generalizations are a bad thing; but there is undeniably an imprudent and irresponsible speaking in public. But where moral theologians do not merely love *le dernier cri*, but work both competently and in awareness of their responsibility, one can ask whether the fear of "dangerous confusion" (which certainly can exist) does not sometimes appear rather as an anxiety that a smoothly functioning operation may be disturbed or, even more fundamentally, as a fear of having to speak and teach more responsibly and more credibly. Ought one not then seek a more intensive and more confident cooperation? The initiatives for this can ultimately proceed from both sides: as John Paul II has said, the theologians too should take initiatives.[11]

It will be seen, then, that tensions are not to be completely excluded. There is a fear of authority that can lead theologians to keep silent, even when they see that by their silence an important service is withheld from the People of God. Moral theologians, too, have a conscience that demands responsible action. Sometimes a still and careful reservation is more effective in the long term than a loud protest: often a careful and steady sowing of good seed by many hands among the People of God produces new insight and new life, even if only very slowly.

But another kind of behavior can suggest itself. In the notorious case of Savonarola, a cardinal publicly admonished the Master of the Sacred Palace, Pier Paolo Giannerini (a Dominican like Savonarola) not to defend Savonarola so energetically, but to defend the Holy See. He received the reply: "My commission is to fight for the truth, and in this way to safeguard the honor of the Holy See."[12] If all dissent in the Church were excluded, nothing could ever be corrected; one thinks, for example, of religious freedom.[13] Some time ago, H. Fries wrote (even though not specifically about moral theologians) that one must require of the theologian "the courage for criticism, for nonconformity" too, "especially when this is not conditioned by the need for prestige and vanity, but by responsibility for the task entrusted to theology."[14] (Must one point out specifically that, like moral theologians, bishops too who share the concerns of moral theologians can get into difficult situations with regard to official episcopal declarations or authoritative decrees?) Several years ago, the Canadian theologian F.E. Crowe, S.J., asked himself publicly whether the theologians' silence about the famous "Washington Case" had not made them guilty of failure to aid the priests and many laypersons affected by it.[15]

If a serious moral-theological attempt to stretch out a helping hand to the People of God runs the risk of creating the apparent impression of "confusion" among Christians who are unprepared or who are concerned about their inherited security, may not the present moment call for a common dialogue between bishops and moral theologians that works to establish insight and mediate understanding? In certain circumstances, however, it may be that what appears as "confusion" is in reality the long overdue beginning of a rethinking.

II. TEACHING AUTHORITY AND MORAL-THEOLOGICAL PROBLEMATIC

A certain lack of cooperation and a corresponding tension between bishops and moral theologians are determined, *inter alia*, by pressing complexes of moral-theological problems; for neither scholarly moral theology nor ecclesiastical direction can be merely the repetition of what has already been said. It is indeed the case that what is true is always true; but one cannot deduce from this the existence of a block of definitive moral insights, once and for all "possessed" and so "to be handed on," for such a conception would make a mockery of the history of Christianity. In every age there are untruths (errors that are given out as truths), half-truths, attempts at reasoning which fall short, etc., and these challenge to renewed reflection. But, independently of this, man (mankind), and Christian man too, never ceases to reflect on what really exists, on how he leads his life, how he can give content to his life, and how he should make concrete decisions. This is so, simply in that he is a man and a Christian, but also in that he realizes his humanity and Christianity always under the given circumstances, states of information, and valuations of particular periods and cultures.

The first consequence of this is that within moral theology there always is, and must be, a fresh insight, understanding, evaluation, and judgment. It is readily understandable that not all moral theologians in a particular cultural constellation will agree immediately about everything. Naturally, the situation of the "moral" magisterium in the Church too is affected by this—and is not made easier thereby. A second consequence of what has been said is that bishops who are not themselves active moral theologians can often acquaint themselves only to an insufficient degree with the complex new problems that arise. Thereby their episcopal service of unity in truth becomes harder. It will not be easy to meet this situation of need. In what follows, we shall attempt to expand what has already been said by tackling briefly three acute issues that generate problems in the realm of Catholic moral theology.

1. Moral Goodness and Correctness. The first set of problems which experience shows creates anxiety for many bishops (and other Christians) concerns the possibility (to use a simple formulation) of distinguishing between good and evil. The question that causes concern runs as follows: have not today's moral theologians made it very hard for the Church—the people of the Church and the bishops—to distinguish still, openly and clearly, between good and evil? If this were so, this situation would have to be regarded as very serious. But if it is fundamentally a matter of a different, less significant problem, then one would have to judge otherwise. In fact, not only many believers but also certain moral theologians and indeed many bishops, have not yet sufficiently realized a distinction that has been more clearly worked out in contemporary moral theology than it was in earlier epochs; hence many misunderstandings and anxieties arise.

Here it is the distinction between the concepts good and evil, and the concepts right and wrong, that is insufficiently differentiated and thus often confused; more precisely, it is the distinction between personal goodness and badness, on the one hand (the *person* is good or evil), and the moral rightness and wrongness of behavior in the world, on the other hand (the *behavior* of the personal human being is right or wrong). But since personal goodness or badness is much more oriented toward the act of Christian faith than the right or wrong realization of the world of man, and since the episcopal concern is correspondingly directed primarily to personal moral goodness and only secondarily to morally right behavior in the world, the insufficient distinction between the two spheres can lead to striking misunderstandings and predicaments.

A few years ago, the German translation of the Lord's Prayer (with the sympathetic knowledge of the bishops) altered the petition for deliverance from "evil/sin." The first concern of the Christian who pays heed to his salvation, and of the bishops who care for this salvation, is not freedom from all evil, even from the evil in the world that is caused by man through wrong behavior, but the freedom from *personal moral evil,* from *sin;* that is, to put it positively, a concern for personal moral *goodness.* Without personal moral goodness, i.e., the moral goodness of the person, faith would be without love and life, and hence dead. Relative certainty about right behavior vis-à-vis the goods or values of this world (a good thing—but not necessarily personal goodness) and its difference from humanly wrong conduct (an evil—but not necessarily personal evil), are therefore of great value. Such awareness, as the Christian understands it, is to be sought wherever possible; indeed it has repeatedly been sought in the Christian Church and, with varying success, has been found with sufficient certainty; but it does not determine personal moral goodness. It is not the rightness of our behavior in the world that belongs to the essence of personal moral goodness, but loyal adherence to what one is able to take for the right behavior. Uncertainties about personal moral goodness are essentially different from uncertainties about the rightness of behavior toward the goods of the world.

Believing Christians and their bishops should not allow themselves to be unnecessarily confused by misleading and often polemical laments or accusations; for with regard to the decisive distinction between good and evil—i.e., in the realm of personal morality—there are no uncertainties and divergences of opinion in contemporary moral theology. It is universally acknowledged that one may not act against a responsibly formed conscience; that one must always be morally good in one's decisions and may never be evil; that one should always respect and treat every human being as a person; that one must avoid, as far as possible, innerworldly evils in the realization of the world of man; that in the realization of the innerworldly reality one must proceed in justice, mercy, generosity, chastity, etc. (to the extent that one is able to recognize what justice, chastity, etc. concretely demand); that one may never employ something that is morally disallowed as a means to attain a good goal. It seems to be important to point out this final item, because the representatives of contemporary moral theology are often accused (falsely) of stating the opposite.[16]

As one may understand from the new formulation of the petition in the Lord's Prayer, a different kind of language is required for speaking of the distinction between right and wrong in the realization of the innerworldly reality than is required for speaking of the distinction between good and evil in personal morality. Because this is often overlooked, misunderstandings and "confusions" easily happen. This is all the more astonishing, in that a traditional formulation (even though an unhappy one) teaches the distinction and the possible non-coincidence of "formal" (personal) and "only material" sin. "Only material sin" is, however, a very bad formulation, for sin implies precisely the opposite of personal goodness. "Material sin" means what a better formulation calls, not "sin" at all, but "wrong behavior" in the realization of the innerworldly reality. It is only by analogy to personal moral evil that this wrongness is also called "moral" wrongness (because if one were aware of it—and one is obliged to strive for this awareness—its realization in freedom would represent moral evil, and hence personal sin).

If this is taken into account, if it is truly grasped that the question of "right or wrong" in the realization of the earthly reality of man-society-world is not the primary problematic of personal morality, but the secondary (though also very important) question of what kind of behavior in this earthly reality best corresponds to this human innerworldly reality, then it will perhaps be more easily seen that the solution to the problems of right or wrong behavior in the construction of the world—i.e., to the problem of norms of innerworldly behavior—will be neither easy nor uniform; nevertheless, it is not so urgent that it requires the "absolute," "universal," "*intrinsece malum*" character that applies to the realm of good/evil personal morality.

In concrete living, however, and for practical morality, the question of right/wrong in daily behavior is urgent, since moral goodness demands a striving for the best behavior possible. In the case of the problematic of right/wrong, unlike the more important problematic of good/evil, there are some statements of contemporary moral theology which could at first sight "confuse" one who knows only the moral theology of a particular period (without, however, knowing the variations in the history of moral theology). Where do the causes of such a "confusion" and of a corresponding reservation vis-à-vis today's moral theologians lie? To overcome such a reservation, should one not take the trouble to consider whether it may be possible to come to an understanding in some fundamental statements?

We may take as examples the following statements. 1. The pluriformity and mutability of earthly and historical realities have led in the past to judgments about the moral rightness of concrete behavior that were not the same in all periods. To take only one example in a field that oddly enough is repeatedly of prominent concern, sexual ethics: recent studies seem to establish that, on the one hand, intercourse within marriage, if practiced out of motives other than procreation, was for centuries held to be a sin, while the phenomenon of masturbation, unlike many other questions in sexual ethics, was not dealt with by moral theologians for about the first five centuries.

2. As Thomas Aquinas emphasized, it is a mistake to think that concrete actions can be completely resolved through the application of abstract norms (and not through the "*extensio*" that implies new insight).

3. The lack of sufficient explanations of the reasons for norms of behavior, i.e., the inability to make them comprehensible, can cause doubts about the rightness of such norms. This problem arose, for example, in the *propositiones* presented to the Pope at the 1980 Synod of Bishops in the case of two important problems (contraception and the reception of the sacraments by divorced and remarried persons).

4. The well-known appeal to the "nature of the case" for particular norms can help bring about recognition of the structure of man (as personal, interpersonal, etc.) and the "laws of nature" (physiology, psychology, physics and chemistry, the finalities of nature, etc.). Yet the "nature" of particular realities cannot, as such, be the measure applied to discover right behavior. This measure is rather human reason, which examines the data of nature in the whole context of man's personal reality and thus can make a normative judgment about right human behavior. The false conclusion *ex natura rei* has long been denounced by many ethicists, and this has been more and more acknowledged even within Catholic moral theology, but it can still be found in statements of the Church's magisterium, and limits their credibility within and outside the Church's fellowship.

5. The problematic of the universal validity and applicability of humanly formulated norms of behavior should be recognized as a serious problematic. If one cannot go along with the "naturalistic fallacy" of the *"ex natura rei,"* one must argue teleologically through consideration of innerworldly (and thus not absolute) goods and ills of man's personal world. This does not totally exclude the possibility of coming to universal negative norms of behavior (*"intrinsece malum"*), but only on condition that one takes appropriate account of all the given, and even possible, morally relevant objectives, effects, and circumstances in them, for only thus is there a guarantee of full objectivity and universality. This presupposition is fulfilled only if further possible elements in a formulation are excluded (e.g., "do not kill, *only* because it pleases someone so," "do not pay an insufficient wage, *only* for the sake of one's own enrichment," the rightness of a particular act, e.g., the payment of a family wage, "in the given situation *at the present moment"*, etc.). The many norms of behavior which are not formulated thus can give significant practical help, but scarcely exclude the theoretical possibility that further additional and morally relevant elements, if these have not already been sufficiently taken into consideration, may determine a different judgment of moral rightness, and this can have effects *in praxi* too.

2.   *Faith and Morals.*   A second set of problems is closely connected to the first. Christian faith has much to contribute to the question of the Christian's personal moral goodness, but questions of the rightness of innerworldly behavior do not have the same support from faith. This means that one who feels obliged to cast doubts upon certain concrete moral behavioral norms that are maintained in the Church does not thereby sin directly against his faith. Yet we constantly hear that Christians are bound by the fact of their being Christians to particular norms of behavior. This could be taken to mean that these norms in the whole of their content have their basis in Christian faith. Bishops must protect not only themselves, but their faithful, too, from such an error.

In accordance with the tradition of moral theology, in point of fact, it is not the Christian faith, but the *recta ratio* (the right judgment of reason) that is the norm of behavior in the world. This *"recta" ratio* must be established through the human *"ratio"* (reason), and this reason, in order not to stray all too easily from the *"recta ratio"* (truth), receives help (according to Vatican II) through "the light of the gospel"; thus it is always still reason itself, "illuminated", it is true, "by the faith", and not simply the Christian faith itself that must establish what constitutes right behavior in this world. This is basically the traditional teaching of the natural moral law (even though this has not always been understood in the same sense). If there is discussion today among moral theologians about "ethics of faith" and "autonomous moral theology in the Christian context," the bishops should think not so much of Kant but of Christian teaching about natural law, when they hear the words *"autonomous* moral theology."* It is rather the concept "ethics of *faith"* that should make the bishops concerned about the loss of the Christian teaching on natural law that tradition has maintained. This is not opposed to the fact that the establishment of what is morally right always takes place within the one act of Christian faith.[17]

I am grateful to Hans Urs von Balthasar's *Theology of History* (published many years before his *Nine Theses on Christian Ethics* were published by Joseph Ratzinger in 1975) for the idea that the moral *ratio recta* of the moral natural law is based more deeply in Jesus Christ than in the *ratio* itself.[18] In this sense, a *recta ratio* exists for us finally within personal faith in Jesus Christ.

But because human reason (even that of Christians) can make judgments about moral behavior only under human and historical conditions and so only with "moral certainty," it frequently happens, for example, in episcopal statements, that the supposedly "more certain" appeal back to the Bible occurs, whether to the Ten Commandments, to the Sermon on the Mount, or to Paul. It is here that one hopes to find definitive certainty, or rather, security. But how justified is this?

When the ecclesial document, *Persona humana*, on certain questions of sexual ethics was published in 1975, certain German moral theologians lamented that its uncritical and hermeneutically unsatisfactory treatment of scriptural texts was no longer defensible by scholars today. When H. Schürmann made his contribution as an exegete, in the booklet of J. Ratzinger already mentioned, to the defense of an "ethics of faith,"[19] his final argument was that words of the Lord and of scripture can demand only an "approximate carrying-out . . . in accordance with the situation."

When several episcopal directives appealed without further explanations to the fifth commandment in the discussion about abortion and the death penalty, certain questions inevitably arose, though the faithful and even some bishops seemed unaware of them: first of all, whether the word "kill" or only "murder" was germane to the Ten Commandments, and second, whether the condemnation of abortion and the death penalty were directly expressed in the commandment or only "along the lines of" the fifth commandment; and beyond this, whether an historical speaking or writing by God, or another theologically important event, accounted for the significance of the fifth commandment.[20]

When the American and German bishops had to give an answer recently to the pressing problems of peace and war, they had to face the question whether the Sermon on the Mount intended to introduce from above the absolutely new requirement of nonviolence into the history of mankind, or whether the Sermon intended only to admonish self-seeking mankind (in its varied manifestations: Jewish limitation of the full moral truth, Gentile misbehavior, tax collectors and sinners) to obey the requirement of love and mutual consideration already in force— though without spelling out clearly what this might mean in concrete cases. There is a danger in all these cases that one may take a one-sided attitude, deriving from the "ethics of faith," in a search for security about innerworldly behavior which this ethics cannot justify.

3.   Competence and Authority.   In order to be able to make valid statements about the various problems of morally defensible behavior (i.e., correct innerworldly behavior), it is obvious that a corresponding competence is required, in order to understand and judge the material problems which are always contained in such issues. A corresponding authority is also necessary, in order to make official statements about correct innerworldly behavior in the Christian community. Bishops and moral theologians both stand, in their different ways, before the double problem of competence and authority.

The competence required for corresponding statements is basically the same for bishops and for moral theologians (and other Christians). They can and must seek from appropriate sources the necessary information about the reality and implications of the use of nuclear weapons and of modern warfare in general, or about the scientific issues in modern genetics, or about the actualities of marriage in all its variety—to name only a few examples—if they intend to make a moral statement in each of these areas. They can and must master in the same way the knowledge of fundamental moral principles which is required to make such statements.

The question arises, however, whether a specifically episcopal authority is involved in such statements, that is, not only the question of a specific mission, but also of a specific "assistance" of the Holy Spirit corresponding to such a mission.[21] The answer must be affirmative but this does not necessarily mean the specific "assistance in questions of faith and morals," guaranteeing infallibility in certain circumstances, of which the First Vatican Council spoke. If the assistance of the Spirit is guaranteed to the Church as a whole, it is guaranteed also to the individual missions. But that includes the theologians as well, especially when they have received an official commission; they too have the authority that corresponds to their competence and to their mission in the Church.

The special mission and authority (not competence) of the bishops to establish the Church's unity in truth can fundamentally justify not only instruction, but also intervention against errors. This does not exclude moral theologians from the right and indeed obligation to take similar action; in principle, this could even include admonishing the bishops.

The question of what circumstances oblige bishops not merely to give positive instructions, but even to issue reprimands, is very delicate. They must be certain of the facts of the case; they must also bear in mind that concrete questions *de moribus* are usually not questions of faith, but questions of the natural law that must be established by reasoning, and that the two Vatican Councils did not speak in the same manner of all moral questions of the natural law when they used the formulation "in matters of faith and morals."

While the teaching of the two Councils does not exclude all dissent from officially ("authentically") but not "infallibly" presented teachings, the new Canon Law emphasizes the duty of the bishops to care for a corresponding unity in the Church's fellowship (including, therefore, the fellowship of moral theologians and bishops!) even in questions of (faith and) morals which are not presented infallibly. Canon 810 §2 vaguely requires the bishops to take care that "the principles of Catholic doctrine are faithfully maintained" in Catholic (and ecclesiastical: Canon 919) universities and faculties, but Canon 1371, 1 provides for the punishment of those who uphold a teaching condemned by the pope or by a council, or who reject a teaching taught by the authentic teaching authority of the pope or the college of bishops—even when no "infallible" statement is involved. According to Canon 753, the individual bishops, the episcopal conferences, and particular episcopal synods also exercise an "authentic magisterium," to which the faithful (including the moral theologians) must respond by a "religious readiness" (*obsequium religiosum*) to accept the teaching.

The authority and mission of the bishops to care for ecclesial unity seem to be clearly described here. What of care for the truth? Inasmuch as this care can be presumed in the case of the Church's statements, yes; but inasmuch as the viability of this presumption is not clearly established in every case (in noninfallible declarations), it is obvious that very precarious situations (according to the canonical situation we have set out) can arise.

The question has become freshly acute in the pastoral letters on peace and war which have been issued this year by the North American and the German bishops, and in the period of preparation of these documents.

1. In January 1983 (according to available reports), in the course of a meeting in the Vatican of representatives of several episcopal conferences which preceded the definitive publication, Cardinal J. Ratzinger, as leader of the discussion, warned that episcopal conferences as such have no *mandatum docendi*[22] (hence, only the individual participating bishops have this; but cf. also the new Codex, Canon 753, already quoted), and also that the

bishops should apply their moral teaching concretely, but not in such a way that the magisterium would go beyond common moral principles to exercise pressure on the conscience in the case of individual political decisions.[23]

2. In their definitive letters, both episcopal conferences themselves drew attention to the various degrees of authority of various statements in their own documents. The statement of the Second Vatican Council mentioned above[24] is fundamental: despite their common faith and equal conscientiousness, Christians can come to different conclusions in many concrete questions about the construction of reality. Thus, the American bishops hold both tendencies that exist today in the Church, the more pacifist and the other "classical" tendency, to be justifiable.

Besides this, the American bishops distinguish a threefold authority of various statements in their pastoral letter: authority in general moral principles, in the Church's teachings, and in concrete applications. Precisely in the last case, they observe that they (the bishops) express their opinion (unlike the German bishops), but without wishing thereby to obligate the faithful; as an example, they adduce explicitly their stance on the much debated "first use" of atomic weapons.

The preparation of the American pastoral letter introduced yet another novelty: the preparation took place in the public eye for many months. Not only were specialists in various fields (including departments of the American government) and other episcopal conferences consulted, but reactions to the three successive preliminary drafts were accepted and taken into account. It took a long time for the episcopal conference to produce a text that was accepted by almost all the bishops.

This situation should not be without consequences for the future moral-theological teaching of bishops (and moral theologians).[25]

1. The process of the formation of opinion shows that the understanding of what is correct innerworldly behavior does not always lie at hand, nor is it obvious. It was always (or almost always) true that certain moral theologians were consulted in the preparation of episcopal statements on moral questions: it is obvious now that this consultation should have a broader scope (and include not only moral theologians). A question arises: how certain are the answers after such a long period of preliminary consideration?

2. It can be clearly seen that not all bishops have the same opinion in all questions. They are indeed not obliged to come to a consensus with other bishops. In the case of dissent among the bishops, which bishops should moral theologians and the rest of the faithful listen to? Some years ago, an American bishop insisted in this context that every Catholic must follow the magisterium of his local bishop; is this not a one-sidedly juridical concept of the magisterium?[26] It is right that an authentic magisterium of every bishop is accepted in the Church; but the *obsequium religiosum* which is expected clearly permits many different grades. What is the meaning for episcopal authority, when statements are made on questions of sexual ethics in a pastoral letter of the German bishops in 1973, in a decision of the German Synod in 1975, and likewise in 1975 in a document of the Roman Congregation for the Doctrine of the Faith—but in very different ways?[27]

3. It may not always be quite clear which episcopal statements belong to the first or to the second or to the third of the categories distinguished by the American bishops. The moral theologian will remain aware that episcopal statements may not be presented to an undifferentiated *obsequium religiosum* without distinguishing the various elements.

Tension between bishops and moral theologians is possible; it is not necessary in principle, but must be accepted as a fact of life. The distinct authority of bishops must be understood and seriously considered. Bishops too should acknowledge that not all the positions hitherto defended must be obvious and necessarily free of doubt. Moral theologians too are ready to accept the bishops as the officials responsible for safeguarding unity in truth, and to take them seriously—within the bounds of their official authority. Both sides must strive intensively for an understanding of the mission and situation of the other, and should seek mutual cooperation.

Notes

1. *Readings in Moral Theology, No. 3: The Magisterium and Morality,* ed. by C.E. Curran and R.A. McCormick, S.J., Paulist Press, New York (1982).

2. *Lumen gentium,* no. 25.

3. *Gaudium et spes,* no. 43.

4. Thus, for example, J. Ratzinger, "Theologie und Ethos," in: K. Ulmer, *Die Verantwortung der Wissenschaft*, Bonn (1975), pp. 45–61, on p. 56 criticizes the "mutation of the Christian ethos into an abstract system of natural law"; "more serious still is the ever greater positivism of the thinking of the magisterium, which takes this ethical system in hand and regulates it."

5. *Lumen gentium*, passim.

6. *Gaudium et spes*, nos. 33 and 43.

7. On this and what follows, cf., e.g., A. Dulles, "The Magisterium in History: A Theological Perspective," *Theol. Education* 19 (1983), pp. 7–26; Y. Congar, "Pour une histoire semantique du terme 'magisterium'," *Rev. de sc. phil. et théol.* 60 (1976), pp. 85–98; idem, "Bref historique des formes du 'magistère' et de ses relations avec les docteurs", ibid., pp. 99–112.

8. In: *L'Osservatore Romano*, 1 May 1983, p. 3.

9. Denzinger-Schönmetzer, *Enchiridion*, no. 3884.

10. Cf. Dulles and Congar (note 7).

11. Address to theologians at Altötting, 18 November 1980.

12. Quoted by J.W. O'Malley, "The Fourth Vow in Its Ignatian Context: A Historical Study," *Studies in the Spirituality of Jesuits* 15 (1983, no. 1), p. 17 (with no. 42).

13. One should recall the struggle in the Council about religious freedom before *Dignitatis humanae*.

14. H. Fries, "Die Verantwortung der Theologen für die Kirche," *Stimmen der Zeit* 200 (1982), pp. 245–58, at p. 258.

15. Thus, in W.C. Bier (ed.), *Conscience. Its Freedom and Limitations*, New York (1971), 315 f.

16. For example, this complaint is found in a paper that the American moral theologian G. Grisez forwarded to the American bishops and also to the Vatican, against the second draft of the American Pastoral Letter on peace and war; at the January meeting of the bishops in the Vatican, the Vatican side drew attention to this accusation.

17. K. Demmer repeatedly draws attention in his writings to the unity between the act of faith and the establishment of moral judgments: cf., e.g., "Hermeneutische Probleme der Fundamentalmoral," in: D. Mieth and F. Compagnoni (eds.), *Ethik im Kontext des Glaubens*, Freiburg (1978), pp. 101–19.

18. In: J. Ratzinger (ed.), *Prinzipien christlicher Moral*, Einsiedeln, 2nd ed. (1975), pp. 67–93; idem, *Theologie der Geschichte*, Einsiedeln, 3rd ed. (1959).

19. H. Schürmann, "Die Frage nach der Verbindlichkeit der neutestamentlichen Wertungen und Weisungen," op. cit., pp. 9–39.

20. Cf., as a good synthesis, H. Schüngel-Straumann, *Der Dekalog—Gottes Gebote?*, Stuttgart (1973). Cf. also N. Lohfink, "Die Zehn Gebote ohne den Berg Sinai," in: *Bibelauslegung im Wandel*, Frankfurt (1967), pp. 129–57; F. Scholz, "Um die Verbindlichkeit des Dekalogs—Prinzipien oder Faustregeln?," *Theol. d. Gegenwart* 25 (1982), pp. 316–27; W. Molinski, "Die Zehn Gebote. Eine Grundlage für einen ethischen Konsens unter Glaubenden?," *Stimmen der Zeit* 201 (1983), pp. 53–60. Fundamental: F.L. Hossfeld, *Der Dekalog. Seine späten Fassungen, die originale Komposition und seine Vorstufen*, Göttingen (1982).

21. On what follows, see also my reflections "Sittliche Wahrheiten—Heilswahrheiten?", *Stimmen der Zeit* 200 (1982), pp. 662–76 (English translation, Chapter 4 of this book).

22. Cf. *The Tablet*, 30 April 1983. Cf. also the similar-sounding thesis of Archbishop J.F. Whealon, "Magisterium," *Homil. and Past. Rev.* 76 (July 1976), pp. 10–19; on this, R.A. McCormick, *Notes on Moral Theology 1965–1980*, Washington (1981), pp. 658–61.

23. *Herderkorrespondenz* (June 1983), p. 288.

24. *Gaudium et spes*, no. 43.

25. Cf. W. Seibel, "Hirtenbrief in neuem Stil," *Stimmen der Zeit* 201 (1983), pp. 145f.

26. Archbishop Whealon (note 22).

27. Cf. R. Bleistein, "Kirchliche Autorität im Widerspruch," *Stimmen der Zeit* 194 (1976), 145f.

ACKNOWLEDGMENTS

Chapter 1, "Christian Ethics in a Secular Arena." Public lecture, Georgetown University, Washington, D.C., 1982.

Chapter 2, "Christianity, Christian Ethics, and the Crisis of Values." Public lecture, Pontifical Gregorian University, Rome, 1980; The Catholic University of America, Washington, D.C., 1982, etc.

Chapter 3, "Moral Truth—between Objectivism and Subjectivism." German original, *Gregorianum* 63 (1982), 631–46.

Excursus, "Hermeneutics in Ethics and Law." Communication (in German) to the Symposium "Recht als Sinn und Institution," Salzburg, 18–20 May, 1983, organized by the Institute of Jurisprudence of the University of Salzburg; publication in preparation.

Chapter 4, "Moral Truths—Truths of Salvation?" German text in *Stimmen der Zeit* 200 (1982), 662–76.

Chapter 5, "Intrinsically Evil Acts"? Report to an international study week for moral theologians on the universality and immutability of moral norms, Rome, 1981. Public lecture at the University of California, Berkeley, 1982. German text in: *Sittliche Normen. Zum Problem ihrer allgemeinen und unwandelbaren Geltung*, ed. W. Kerber, Düsseldorf, 1982, 74–91.

Chapter 6, "Nature and Culture in Bioethics." Communication to a symposium of moral theologians on the concept of nature, at Castel Gandolfo (Rome), 7–9 October 1983.

Chapter 7, "Human Authority—between the Sacral and the Secular." Complete revision of "Auctoritas Dei in auctoritate civili," *Periodica de re mor., can., lit.* 52 (1963), 3–18; German in *Gregorianum* 64 (1983), 669–82.

Chapter 8, "Faith, Ethics, Law." German lecture at the Symposium "Das Naturrechtsdenken heute und morgen," Salzburg, 5–8 October 1982; published in: *Naturrechtsdenken heute und morgen*, eds. D. Mayer-Maly and P. Simons, Berlin, 1983, 751–62.

Chapter 9, "Teaching Morality: The Tension between Bishops and Theologians within the Church." German text in *Stimmen der Zeit* 201 (1983), 601–19.

8613